The Pocket Mentor for Game Production

Want to work as a producer in the video games industry? Then this is the book for you. This book provides all the essential information and guidance you need to understand the industry and get your foot on the ladder.

This book covers everything from basics you'll need to understand, how to look for and apply for job opportunities, as well as the studio interview process itself. It also includes advice for what to do once you're in the role, with chapters covering the day-to-day of working as a game producer, how to set goals for future career progression, as well as interviews with top tips from experts in the industry.

This book will be of great interest to all beginner and aspiring game producers.

Doug Pennant is a game industry veteran of 13 years, having worked in QA and Production at Microsoft, Creative Assembly, and more recently FundamentalVR. Amidst the complexities of game production pipelines, he developed a particular focus on the growth and development of colleagues and the improvement of game production as a craft. He is deuteranopic color-blind and has given a number of industry talks and workshops on accessibility in video games, including a talk at the 2019 Game Developer Conference (GDC) on designing for color-blindness in games.

The Pocket Mentors for Games Careers Series

The Pocket Mentors for Games Careers provide the essential information and guidance needed to get and keep a job in the modern games industry. They explain in simple, clear language exactly what a beginner needs to know about education requirements, finding job opportunities, applying for roles, and acing studio interviews. Readers will learn how to navigate studio hierarchies, transfer roles and companies, work overseas, and develop their skills.

The Pocket Mentor for Video Game Writers
Anna Megill

The Pocket Mentor for Video Game Testing
Harún Ali

The Pocket Mentor for Game Community Management
Carolin Wendt

The Pocket Mentor for Animators
Hollie Newsham

The Pocket Mentor for Game Audio
Greg Lester and Jonny Sands

The Pocket Mentor for Video Game UX UI
Simon Brewer

The Pocket Mentor for Game Production
Doug Pennant

For more information about this series, please visit: https://www.routledge.com/The-Pocket-Mentors-for-Games-Careers/book-series/PMGC

The Pocket Mentor for Game Production

Doug Pennant

CRC Press
Taylor & Francis Group
Boca Raton London New York

CRC Press is an imprint of the
Taylor & Francis Group, an **informa** business

Designed cover image: Dr. Victor Jeganathan

First edition published 2025
by CRC Press
2385 NW Executive Center Drive, Suite 320, Boca Raton FL 33431

and by CRC Press
4 Park Square, Milton Park, Abingdon, Oxon, OX14 4RN

CRC Press is an imprint of Taylor & Francis Group, LLC

ISBN: 9781032856261 (hbk)
ISBN: 9781032785608 (pbk)
ISBN: 9781003519065 (ebk)

DOI: 10.1201/9781003519065

Typeset in Times LT Std
by codeMantra

Contents

Acknowledgments

There is a lot that had to happen for all of the words in this book to reach your eyes, and mine is only a small part in the gathering and compiling of the experiences and lessons that make up this body of advice. Even my own knowledge is a product of the opportunities I have been granted, the conversations I have enjoyed, and the experiences of a fortunate career in video games; my professional life is the work of many people.

First, I would like to directly acknowledge the other game professionals who contributed written content to this book. I'd like to thank Grace Carroll for sharing her insights into the complex relationships between the developers and players of a video game, Joanna Jakubowska for her experience of agile development and story points, Nicklaus Goh for his UX testing and research, Mike Webb for his detailed report on automation QA and testing, Tamara Tirjak for her localization wisdom, and Joanna Skorupa for her heartfelt stories on motivating the people around her. I also wish to greatly thank David Bowman, who not only provided the experience of a long-time veteran of leading game teams but has also been a regular source of advice and encouragement for me since we met at Creative Assembly. Many thanks as well to Dr Victor Jeganathan for the positively joyful cover image he created for this book, which is a delightful homage to the impassioned chaos of game development – despite the challenges of the job, I absolutely love making games with people, and I'm grateful he has been able to encapsulate that love visually.

As well as the purely written content I would like to acknowledge some of the developers who advised my writing on various areas where my experience is a little thin, namely, Thomas Miller, Tamas Rabel, Charlotte Roberts, and Kyle Rodgers, who all helped me accurately represent release management, graphics programming, technical animation, and coding languages, respectively. I must also acknowledge in general the many peers from my days at Microsoft, Creative Assembly, and FundamentalVR, around whom my experiences in this book were gained. All the developers who showed me the heart of game-building, the producers who led my way to managing it, as well as the staff at Creative Assembly who helped me with my earlier speaking opportunities, building my confidence in sharing lessons of my own. This book wouldn't have happened without these opportunities, which built me up as an educator. I must also thank Will Bateman from Taylor & Francis for reaching out and inviting me to contribute to the *Pocket Mentor* series; I might never have had the confidence to approach a publisher all on my own, so thank you Will for inviting me to become an author.

Introduction

Ok, introductions first: hello, aspiring Producer! Thank you for picking up this book! I'm Doug, a long-time player and producer of video games. Having been inspired by many great developers and educators before me I have become passionate about the continuous sharing of knowledge; I have given talks on color-blindness, lectured on game audio, and made videos about game production, but for the first time I will be condensing my knowledge into book form, so the next generation of game producers can hit the ground running.

My own interest in video games goes back about as long as I can remember. Growing up I had three different friends who I would visit to play games, one with a Nintendo Entertainment System, one with a Sega Mega Drive, and the other with a PC that could just about run *The Journeyman Project*. Whenever I could I would be visiting them to play games like *MIG 29, Streets of Rage, Simon the Sorcerer,* and so on. I was 15 years old the first time I actually helped on a game when my friend asked for some music for his flash game, *Space Snail*. I wrote the music in MIDI, but we didn't know how to export it to an actual sound file, so we used his tiny MP3 player microphone to just record it directly from the computer speaker. The idea of creating music for games drew me irretrievably toward game development, and in 2010 I joined Microsoft as a game tester working on *Fable 3* for the Xbox360.

Having initially joined the industry through a passion for audio, I was drawn toward production when I realized I *enjoyed* planning, organizing, and making big things happen with talented people. I would always organize group holidays, weekly badminton sessions, and some pretty good house parties. It wasn't until 2015 that this became clear to me as a skill-set, after I had found myself enjoying the management of audio game testers on *Alien: Isolation*. At the beginning of 2016, after applying internally at Creative Assembly for an Associate Development Manager role I got my first production gig where, to start with, I had virtually no idea what I was doing.

This book is everything I have learned since; all the hindsight I have acquired, all the advice I have been given, and all the tricks I have developed to help teams work well together and make great games. Hopefully you can engage with the lessons in these pages, work them into your career right from the start, and go on to build better teams that make better games than ever before.

Success criteria
The goals of this book

1

One of the things I will be preaching throughout this book is about setting clear goals, and I intend to practice what I preach. This chapter will go through why I'm writing this book, what a producer really is, who can take this job on, and the industry in which you will be doing it all.

"WHY?" – THE PURPOSE OF THIS BOOK

My goal with this book is to give the next generation of producers a head start in their career by sharing everything it has taken me more than a decade to learn. With this in mind I have tried to imagine what I would have wanted back when I was first joining both the games industry and the discipline of game production. I had not studied game production or any other kind of project management, instead having studied music technology, game design, and then joined the industry as a game tester. I didn't know what questions to ask about production, so I couldn't even research the answers.

Production is so varied that even the most experienced producer does not have experience with every problem, so my peers often didn't have the answers to my questions. Additionally, game development is an ever-evolving industry, so the problems a new producer faces will never be exactly the same. A junior producer 25 years from now may likely have questions about getting started with AI-driven scheduling software, for which I (currently) have no good answers.

What I would have wanted in the beginning is a high-level crash course in everything "producer," to prime my brain for the types of projects, tasks, people, and tools I had in my future, and to know the skills I needed to navigate the chaos. This is what I have attempted to provide – a high-level view of the career ahead of you in which I assume as little as possible about your prior knowledge in the aim that you will arrive into the industry with your questions answered, plus a few you haven't even thought of yet.

"WHAT?" – WHAT DOES "PRODUCER" EVEN MEAN?

In practical terms, a game producer is someone who arranges the development of a video game and ensures all team, project, and stakeholder needs are met. They may be the sole producer on a project, or one of a team of dozens. The video game industry adopted the term "producer" from the film and television industries, which serve as a fairly good model for what the role should achieve. In these industries, an executive producer will be engaged by a key stakeholder (such as a publishing house or record label) to arrange the creation of a quality product. "This is the brief, this is the budget, this is the deadline. Go make it happen." They will then hire a core team to help flesh out the project, such as the director, writer, casting director, and production manager. From here they will monitor the project to ensure all production needs are being met; the team is functional, quality is being produced, and budgets are being met. They will also need to respond to any unusual needs; if the film script now requires a banana boat, the producers will now need to pick up the phone and find a banana boat, pronto.

Video game producers have a similar role, but software comes with its own needs; an interconnected software team will need its own technology, platforms, stability, and testing needs met. You may also work on an online game, which adds all the considerations of running a live software service. As a result, game producers have largely become software project managers, adopting similar technologies, methodologies, and language to meet the ubiquitous need of tracking the progress of a video game project.

Even in the same studio (and even on the same game) the role will vary, and you could be expected to do any of the following:

- Arrange ideation sessions and prototype testing
- Devise and present long-term project roadmaps
- Track the day-to-day tasks of a single team
- Schedule localization and translation
- Coordinate contracts for outsourced staff
- Arrange food deliveries to the studio

- Run project-wide retrospectives
- Plan company-wide events
- Own a technology or documentation area
- Coordinate casting and actors for voiceover
- Coordinate musicians for soundtrack recording
- Coordinate location scouting for photogrammetry trips
- ...and so on and so on

Every new game, tool, or strategy has the chance to create a new need for the team which – as the producer – you must ensure is met, and how you do this will be a little different every time. Whatever is needed, the producer's job is to *make it happen*.

"WHO?" – WHAT KIND OF PEOPLE MAKE GOOD PRODUCERS?

You may be wondering if you are "the right kind of person" to be a game producer. While each producer role is different, there are a lot of common factors that will make up your day, and this can help you figure out whether this is the career that you'll enjoy.

Good communicator

First, all production is about communication, and so all producers will need to be keen communicators. I specifically choose the word "keen" over "good"; you can become a *good* communicator as your career progresses, but what's important right from the start is that you are ready for communication to be your number one responsibility. A common producer day may look like this:

- Start the day by reading a dozen emails
- Daily team meeting
- Write and respond to a flurry of instant messages
- Spend an hour working on reports
- Weekly feature sync meeting
- Weekly department meeting
- Weekly team all-hands meeting, where you present your team's latest content.

As you can see, whatever area of the game you are looking after, your main role will be about communicating that role, so you will need to be comfortable communicating regularly and proactively.

Good problem-solver

Game producers will also need to be problem solvers. Throughout game development, unforeseen problems will constantly arise; tasks will overrun, systems will go down, relationships on the team will fray, etc. The job of the production team is to ensure that no problem goes left unattended, so you will need to adopt the mindset that everything is somehow solvable. Sometimes this will mean chipping in with low-level feature work, moving gear around the office, or gathering information. However, in many cases you will not be able to solve the problem yourself; frequently one of my colleagues will raise an issue to me that is very technical in nature and well beyond my expertise. In these cases, my job isn't to fix the problem directly, but to connect them with the expert that can. Game teams are often dozens or hundreds of people, and so an artist needing tools help may not know the programmer that can help them, so they will look to you to find this out. You will do a lot of this chasing, fixing, and problem-solving at all levels of production; I think of it as removing all the speed bumps from the road in front of your team so they can proceed without hindrance.

Trustworthy

The last requirement of an aspiring game producer is that you are honest and reliable. One of the greatest gifts a producer can bring is to foster trust among the team, and this starts with building your own trust relationships with the people around you. This will mean being honest with both your developers and your bosses whenever there is a problem; if everyone believes that you will always tell them the truth and that you are a reliable source of information, then they will feel secure in the knowledge that they will always know what they need to know. Being reliable also means keeping your word; when a manager asks you to take care of something (e.g., arranging onboarding for a new starter, etc.), make sure that you do it. If for some reason you can't help, then make sure you communicate this up front, so they know to find another person to handle it. It's essential that people on the team can look to production as a source of trusted information and support, and you can build this through honesty and reliability.

By no means does this list cover every trait that will help production. Some production roles will require you to have a good head for numbers, others a good head for words and languages, and others a degree of design skill. These responsibilities will be explored as the traits of a "communicator" and a "problem-solver" and "honest and reliable" are the ones I see as essential to every single production role.

"WHERE?" – THE VIDEO GAME INDUSTRY TODAY

Before diving into the role of the producer, we should look at the context for the role in the industry today. Video games have come a long way since 1958, when William Higinbotham first displayed an interactive oscilloscope exhibit called *Tennis for Two* at the Brookhaven National Laboratory in Upton, New York.[1] From a single queue of people in a New York laboratory the player base of video games has grown to over 3.2 billion people in 2024[2] and has spread from the humble oscilloscope to the television in your living room, the computer in your office, the mobile phone in your pocket, and even *strapped to your face* in the wake of recent strides in virtual reality headsets. From individual hobbyist "game-writers" (the original term for solo developers), we now have multiskilled development teams numbering thousands of people in multinational corporations connecting multiple studios working on a single title.

Many studios are now owned by an array of huge publishing companies that fund and produce the biggest video games, building multiyear strategies that tie together games, movies, TV shows, events, and merchandise all under a single IP. If you watch the credits on a modern game, you may be sitting through a slowly scrolling list of hundreds of people from dozens of studios across several countries. Where games used to be made by a single "game writer," many game jobs are now highly – almost *absurdly* – specialized; I knew one animator who had a full-time job animating horses in *Total War*, and a coder whose main responsibility on *Alien: Isolation* was modeling the sight and sound perception systems of the alien. These specializations are usually in the service of an established genre of games (e.g., shooters, strategies, RPGs, etc.) to try and build a highly profitable game production pipeline, with as much guaranteed return on investment as they can secure.

Bigger production lines have helped games grow from having one or two players on a single screen in an arcade to communities of thousands, all sharing the same virtual space. When Blizzard launched *World of Warcraft* in 2004, a game with a persistent world in which millions of players could all participate, the industry developed the term "massively multiplayer online role-playing game," or MMORPG for short (or MMO for *even* shorter). The communities surrounding these games grew enormously and brought players together like never before. Other game communities grew around the competitive nature of the title; players would arrange tournaments of games like *Street Fighter* and *Unreal Tournament*, which over time would build a dedicated following of players, fans, and organizers. Now, players of games like *Starcraft*, *League of Legends,* and *Counter-Strike: Global Offensive* compete in internationally broadcast tournaments for cash prizes and global recognition, leading to "eSports" becoming a household phrase.

The release of smartphones has caused the mobile game industry to explode, with thousands of studios embracing the platform. Mobile games generate almost half the game industry's revenue (49% as of 2024[3]), with tile-matching games like *Candy Crush: Saga* and role-playing games like *Genshin: Impact* racking up millions of players worldwide. These studios will endlessly experiment with the interface of their games, gathering and analyzing vast quantities of interaction, retention, and revenue data to further and further hone the financial effectiveness of their titles.

Despite this growth, there are still many independent – better known as "indie" – game developers around the world, often in teams as small as one, building games in their own time, often with no real guarantee of a financial return. Developing with lower financial risk allows these developers to take more risks with the nature of the game itself; recent titles like *Return of the Obra Dinn, Chants of Senaar,* and Unpacking all showcase unique game mechanics, respectively, using attention-to-detail, language decoding, and the simple unpacking of boxes to tell a compelling story. New game development tools such as Unreal Editor, Unity, and Game Maker have made it easier than ever for smaller teams to create and release games, and have enabled people without programming knowledge to express themselves through interactive media.

Even now it's highly unlikely we have seen the final form of video games. Modern tinkerers and inventors continue to explore the possibility of interactive media, such a Robin Baumgarten's *Line Wobbler,* a one-dimensional platform game played on a lighting tube, or Jerry Belich's *Choosatron, a* choose-your-own adventure game where the display is not a screen but a printed receipt, which you can tear off and keep when you finish. The internet has allowed for wild experiments to take place, such as *Twitch Plays Pokemon*, an online event in which all viewers of a twitch stream would simultaneously control a single game of *Pokémon Red*, with the concurrent viewer count peaking at 120,000.[4]

The game industry has also courted the realm of augmented reality (AR) games, in which the player's real world location is integral to the game mechanics. Niantic's mobile game *Ingress* laid the foundations for global participation AR games such as their subsequent release, *Pokémon GO*, which had an estimated 200 million monthly players at its peak.

In summary, the game industry is a wild and ever-changing beast, and as a producer you will need to be ready to navigate this evolving landscape, shepherding your teams through the changing environment to find success together.

DAVID BOWMAN – CHIEF OPERATING OFFICER AT XR GAMES

We didn't used to have producers – we used to just get together, make something fun and then ship it. In the early days you'd go to a publisher with a completed, fun game, and the request was 'help us sell it'. Then the company would say "make us a sequel," and now there were new expectations, which means you needed to plan for them, communicate the progress being made towards them, and manage the new relationships between studio, publisher and audience. Now you needed people who were experts in this field – producers.

One of the big challenges of production is managing this change from organically grown companies into managed sustainable companies without killing them. It's a total change of culture from a company that doesn't understand and measure itself, but never needed to meet a specific target, into something that meets its targets. You have to not kill the "secret sauce," which is hard when no-one knows what it is. A good producer holds up a mirror to the company, and then lets the company identify its hidden knowledge. There is always a lot of knowledge, somewhere in the company, but the risk is that the person with this knowledge will leave, and then the company loses its strengths.

One of the essential roles of production is documenting this institutionalized knowledge so that it isn't lost when people leave, which is getting even more and more of a risk as industry veterans age out of the industry and take their knowledge with them. I've worked at 12 companies, and every company I've worked at has assumed that every other company works the same way. They are all re-inventing the same wheel at the same time, coming up with their own acronyms for the same things, and new solutions for the same old problems. It also means they have to re-learn everything all over again. This is where producers are again important, as someone needs to do the job of studying these processes and communicating with the other organizations to understand how to interact with them.

Documents and processes can last longer than games. When working on The Climb, I advised 72 frames per second as a minimum requirement for our game on the Oculus Rift. Nine years later, without my further involvement, this has become the standard on the entire Meta VR product line. This is the value of documenting what you discover, as this knowledge escapes, and your good work can become the new normal in the still-maturing industry. Then it can be up to the creatives and story-tellers to find all these new spaces in magic and wonder and adventure.

REFERENCES

1. Wikipedia contributors. Tennis for Two [Internet]. Wikipedia, The Free Encyclopedia. 2024. Available from: https://en.wikipedia.org/w/index. php?title=Tennis_for_Two&oldid=1243756129
2. Dimitrievski M. Gaming statistics 2024 [Internet]. TrueList. 2022 [cited 2024 Sep 9]. Available from: https://truelist.co/blog/gaming-statistics/
3. Newzoo.com. [cited 2024 Sep 9]. Available from: https://newzoo.com/resources/ blog/global-games-market-revenue-estimates-and-forecasts-in-2024
4. Wikipedia contributors. Twitch Plays Pokémon [Internet]. Wikipedia, The Free Encyclopedia. 2024. Available from: https://en.wikipedia.org/w/index. php?title=Twitch_Plays_Pok%C3%A9mon&oldid=1244762528

Who's who?
Meet the teams

2

When you join a team as a new producer, you are joining as an expert in people and processes, so one of the first things you should do is get to know the people around you. This book is no different; throughout these chapters, I will be referring to many different teams, parties, and individuals, so it will help to know who these all are ahead of time. So, let's meet your fellow game developers…

GAME DESIGN

Game designers are the people who come up with the rules and interactions that make something a "game." These are people who will take a world, a system, or a story and turn it into a set of quests, challenges, and contests. They are driven by the exploration of ideas, and the creation of compelling and satisfying player experiences.

In a small game you will often just have one designer for the whole game, but with larger and more diverse games, we are seeing more and more varied specializations of designer. Here are a few common types as of 2024:

- **Combat designer** – Designs and balances the combat mechanics.
- **Level designer** – Designs and blocks out the first version of a playable game environment.
- **Narrative designer** – Figures out the expression of a story through gameplay mechanics.
- **System designer** – Creates systems in which gameplay occurs, such as crafting, magic, and inventory management.
- **Puzzle designer** – Designs puzzle interactions which range from color-matching to complex lock-picking and more.
- **Economy designer** – Designs in-game systems of money, markets, and trade.

DOI: 10.1201/9781003519065-2

- **Monetization designer** – Identifies game elements for which the player can be charged real money, often designing an in-game currency such as the v-bucks in *Fortnite*.
- **Technical designer** – Develops and maintains tools for designers, and sometimes handles more script/code-based design implementation.

The production team will need to manage designers in preproduction when prototyping the game, the systems and the levels, and finding the mechanics. Later on, the production team will need to ensure they are scheduled to complete each system as planned, and to have time near the end of the game for polishing, balancing, and bug-fixing.

UX (USER EXPERIENCE)

UX staff are focused specifically on the player's perception and understanding of the game, and how the game communicates to them. It requires a good understanding of player psychology, perception trends, and common behaviors. The team members dealing with UX may officially be UX designers, UX artists, and UX researchers. Regardless, they will be focusing on how the UI, sound, and in-world game interactions are communicated in order to improve the player experience.

NICKLAUS GOH, HEAD OF UX RESEARCH

One of the best ways to improve the player experience is to observe players interacting and providing feedback early during development. This can be done with UX testing/research, which involves playtesting with a sample of suitable players who would be interested in the game, ideally representing the game's target audience. UX testing has the benefit of including both data on player interactions with the game and their feedback on said interactions. The former is a powerful tool not just because of the data collected, but because of the empathy it can create in the team, due to them observing potential player struggles with understanding the mechanics or interacting with the game.

While UX testing can have expected outcomes (e.g., "players understood a game mechanic," "players had trouble interacting with parts of the UI," etc.), some of the most valuable insights are those from unexpected outcomes; players have diverse behaviors and may play the game in completely unexpected ways, or have trouble with simple mechanics that are second-nature to the game team. These unexpected outcomes can be energizing, as they surface hidden friction and frustration points in the game.

UX testing can be facilitated by UX researchers whose responsibilities include collaborating with the team, planning out UX tests, recruiting suitable players, moderating sessions, analyzing the data, and communicating the results to the team. It is important that UX researchers be as unbiased and scientific as possible when conducting UX tests, as they need to be neutral when interacting with players to avoid influencing player behavior or feedback. If your team or company is small enough that there is no capacity for a dedicated UX researcher, or lacks access to a central UX research team, then the above can be carried out by a mix of UX designers and producers. This is particularly useful when a team or company has just started their journey to UX maturity, as it is a good way to kick-start UX testing. Alternatively, there are external UX research agencies that specialize in offering UX testing services.

WRITERS

In short, game writers write the story of the game. They will devise both the game's plot, setting, history, and characters. These details inform the art and audio teams, and are used as an anchor to keep the game's world-building consistent. The writers also pen the many lines of dialogue, menu texts, audio logs, and lore texts, and will help with fixing text and localization bugs at the end of the project.

Aside from voice lines and written text, writers will often work with narrative designers to work out how their story will be delivered. Here are some examples of game-based storytelling:

- **Player-driven stories** – Narratives that change depending on a player's actions (e.g., a player choice leads to a character death).
- **Costume development** – Evolving player appearance in response to story events/choices (e.g., scarring, torn clothes, red glowing eyes, etc.).
- **Dialogue style** – Changing the character speech patterns to reflect evolution of the story (e.g., more aggressive lines as they suffer more hardship).

- **Environmental storytelling** – Objects in the world implying backstory (e.g., old signs, graffiti, abandoned toys, etc.).
- **Game mechanics** – Evolving a game mechanic to reflect a change in the story (e.g., player moving slower as they age).
- **NPC (nonplayer character) behaviors** – NPCs remember the player's choices, and responding differently (e.g., attacking you if you chose to kill their brother).

The production team ensures that the writers lay out the details of the story early in preproduction, then make sure that all the different story-telling methods are communicated, prototyped, and agreed upon with the development teams. As the project proceeds, they will need to track the completion of all the narrative content while ensuring that the writing team remains available for consultation when the team needs it.

ART

Artists create everything that you can see in the game; all the 3D models, 2D textures, UI graphics, and VFX (visual effects). They are driven by creating beautiful, visually captivating worlds and experiences, and the production team will support them in this vision. Sometimes they will author every asset individually, or they will create kits early on for later assembling (e.g., character kits and environment kits).

As games continue to grow in scale and complexity, so do the specializations for artists. On a small indie game one artist will often do everything, but on large games you will see artists in extremely focused roles. Here are some common examples throughout the industry:

- **Concept artists** – Create the initial ideas, sketches and images that visually fill out the detailed appearance of a character, environment or object (usually in 2D, but sometimes 3D).
- **2D artists** – Create all the two-dimensional assets such as textures, posters, signs, and loading screens.
- **3D artists** – Create all the two-dimensional assets, ranging from skyscrapers, to fighter jets, to goblins, to pieces of fruit.
- **UI artists** – Create the UI assets, such as health bars, inventory menus, and map icons.
- **VFX artists** – Create all the particle effects in the game such as explosions, magic spells, and rain.

- **Lighting artists** – Design and implement the light sources in the game world, such as sunlight, artificial electric lights, and flaming torches.
- **Technical artists** – Create tools to assist artists such as kit assemblers, model importers, and foliage generators. They will have coding and technical experience, and will also help with testing and optimization of art assets.
- **Marketing artists** – Create art for 2D marketing assets such as motion graphics and videos, plus any physical equipment needed at conferences and expos, such as banners, flyers, and pamphlets.

The production team should ensure that the art direction is fully explored, effectively documented and communicated to the art teams during preproduction. They will then schedule and manage the work while arranging for effective review and oversight by the art directors and leads, accommodating any dependencies, and keeping time set aside near the end of the project for optimization, testing, and bug-fixing.

ANIMATION

Once artists have created the characters, items, and settings, it's over to the animators to bring them to life. A single human character in a game can have dozens to hundreds of animations; walking, jumping, crouching, fighting, scratching their head, eating a sandwich, and so on, whatever the game needs. It isn't just the characters that need animations; any items, weapons, and environments that have any kind of movement will need an animator to make it move.

Here are summaries of some of the many skill-sets involved in modern game animation:

- **2D animators** – Create 2D animations such as individual frames for a sprite, or using software to program "tweened" movements.
- **3D animators** – Animate the 3D models, using a mixture of key-frame animations, motion capture data, and animation blending systems.
- **Technical animators** – Combining an understanding of animation methods with the technical skills required to build software tools that help manage animation libraries, state machines, and control rigs. They also generally handle the "rigging" stage of model creation, where digital "bones" are added to a 3D model.

- **Motion-capture (mocap) engineers** – Manage the facilities and technologies required for motion-capture, as well as directing the performances and processing the recorded data to prepare it for use by animators.
- **Motion-capture (mocap) performers** – Physical performers trained in acting and body movement, sometimes specializing in martial arts, dances, and sports. Animals have also been drafted in to perform; dogs provided motion capture for *Call of Duty: Ghosts* and *God of War Ragnarök*, and horses provided motion capture for *Red Dead Redemption 2*.

The production team will need to ensure the animation needs are discussed thoroughly during preproduction, ensuring that necessary expertise, technologies, and mocap facilities are available before these pipelines are committed to. They should then build a schedule that accommodates all of these dependencies, track that work as the project proceeds, and ensure any issues are quickly resolved.

PROGRAMMING

The founders of the video game industry, programmers (aka coders), construct the games tools and digital infrastructures that make video games possible. They will be the primary builders and maintainers of all your systems. In the early days, programmers were coding the visual output pixel by pixel, whereas they now construct "engines" to facilitate easier development by wrapping the complex code functions up in visual interfaces and libraries.

While many programming languages are used in video games, the most common are C++ and C# (pronounced "C plus plus" and "C sharp," respectively). C++ is a "low-level" language which compiles directly to machine code, allowing for better performance, but requires the programmer to manage low-level functions (e.g., memory allocation) more directly. C# is considered a "high-level" language which automatically handles many of those functions, but this comes with the price of harder performance management, and potential compatibility issues when shipping to multiple devices.

The main language is generally chosen at the engine level, for instance, the *Unreal* game engine uses a modified version of C++, while the *Unity* game engine uses C# with bespoke platform compilers to help with compatibility. For a good summary of modern game languages and engines, I recommend the blog post entitled "7 Best Programming Languages for Game Development in 2024" on the website hackr.[1]

On small teams a programmer may create their own game engine from scratch, before moving onto programming the gameplay, the animations, the audio, and the multiplayer all on their own. In contrast, programmers on large teams will be highly specialized. Here are some common specializations of game programmer:

- **Gameplay programmer** – Works on systems for combat, movement, NPC relationships, item crafting, and any other system with which the player interacts directly. They often collaborate closely with the design team.
- **Animation programmer** – Works on animation systems that call, play, interrupt, blend, and tune animations at runtime.
- **Engine programmer** – Build, tune, and develop game engines proprietary game engines, or develop modifications to licensed engines like Unreal, Unity, and Godot.
- **Graphics programmer** – Work on the rendering systems that decide how the game is rendered; how lines are drawn, how colors are managed, how shadows are computed, and so on.
- **UI programmer** – Build systems to drive the UI with gameplay mechanics, such as damage dealt per hit, speeds of vehicles, trajectories of projectiles, and so on.
- **Simulation programmer** – Construct the complex simulations that power the game experience. Simulation examples include the traffic in *Cities: Skylines*, the respawning of forests in *Valheim*, or the flow of sand and water in *From Dust*.
- **Physics programmer** – Program the mathematics of the game's physical world, testing and tuning the physics simulation to create an intuitive environment that the player can manipulate.
- **Artificial intelligence (AI) programmer (NPC behavior)** – Manage the computer-driven NPC behaviors in games, such as soldier search patterns in a stealth game, driving styles of competing cars in a racing game, or the decisions of nations in a strategy game.
- **VFX programmer** – Works with VFX teams to create systems to drive shaders and particle effects from gameplay parameters. They will also work on optimizing any VFX created for the game to manage performance impacts.
- **Audio programmer** – Creates systems to drive the audio via gameplay states and parameters. They also manage environmental audio propagation, sound processing, and optimization.
- **Network programmer** – Handles the connections and data transfer between a player's game and the online environment, be it

another player's client, or a central server. They will create systems to synchronize the desired parameters across the server, handle errors, and flag up any desynchronizations between players.

- **Tools programmer** – Works on software tools to help the developers create assets faster, implement content easier, test game areas, and more.
- **AI programmer (AI technology)** – At the time of writing this is somewhat speculative, but as large-language models, machine learning, stable diffusion, and generative AI are becoming better and more popular, I expect the game industry to heavily invest in these new AI tools for both development and in-game functions. I expect to see a programming discipline focused on these tools develop before long.

Many programmers and code teams are quite self-sufficient in managing their work, but they will be relying on the production team to keep them clearly updated with changes to requirements, priorities, and deadlines, as well as helping them maintain effective communication channels with the rest of the team. Producers should also ensure that any bugs blocking development are communicated immediately to the relevant code team, and see to resolving them quickly.

AUDIO

In his exemplary keynote video for the 2009 Global Game Jam, indie developer Kyle Gabler told the thousands of audience members, "Audio is half the experience, so don't forget about it!"[2] Audio can take a game from an interactive slideshow to a living, breathing world that immerses the player.

In the early days of video games, all the audio was synthesized at runtime by the computer chips in the console, and had to be programmed in, sound by sound. Many modern games, by contrast, have several gigabytes of recorded sound effects, hours of recorded music, and more lines of dialogue than a multi-season TV show. The audio team will need to arrange for recording, editing, and designing of all the audio assets, creating all of the systems that handle the playback, and building an audio experience that matches the narrative, gameplay, and experience goals of the game. Most games these days also use an audio middleware tool – such as Wwise, Fmod, or Elias – as an interface to arrange and script the playback systems for their audio assets.

As with every department, there are some one-person indie studios where a single person handles all the creation and implementation of the audio content, but here is a list of audio specialists you are likely to see working on the larger games:

- **Sound designer** – Creates assets for sound effects and implements them into the game, using a combination of newly recorded sounds, licensed audio libraries, and synthesizers.
- **Dialogue engineer** – Casts actors, prepares scripts, directs the recording sessions, edits the lines, and implements them into the game. Many studios outsource their dialogue casting and recording to specialist companies with the necessary facilities and voice actor contacts.
- **Voice actor** – Performs spoken dialogue lines for all characters and creatures. Usually a contracted professional, and often a member of a union (e.g., SAG-AFTRA in the USA).
- **Music designer** – Creates dynamic music systems using audio middleware tools. These systems will handle tracks, volumes, and transitions at runtime to make the soundtrack feel at one with the gameplay.
- **Composer** – Writes the music for the game, collaborating closely with the music designer and the audio director. A lot of game music is fully synthesized in software, but composers will also use live musician recordings, and may also hire an arranger. Most game composers are freelance.
- **Arranger** – An arranger is someone who is trained in the scoring of music for different types of instruments and can help a composer prepare their written music for orchestral performance.
- **Musician** – A professional player of one or more musical instruments, brought in to record musical parts for the soundtrack.
- **Orchestra** – A musical ensemble of several dozen musicians trained to play classical instruments from a written score. Orchestras are established companies that will often have their own preferred arrangers and recording facilities.

Producers should ensure that all audio goals, budgets, and dependencies are discussed early on. Recording actors and musicians require a lot of lead time, so this needs early planning. During the production phase the sound design team will need to be made aware of any feature changes so they can adjust the audio to respond.

QA

QA stands for quality assurance and is the process of verifying features, stress testing systems, and evaluating the player experience ahead of releasing the game. QA testers will test features in isolation during development, and later on will test the overall experience as if they were an end user, reporting all issues they find to the development team as "bugs." Most studios have a modest-sized internal QA team and will contract large external QA teams during the later phases of development. Publishers will often have their own QA teams, which means they can supply their studios with known, trained testers.

QA titles can vary, and some companies have bespoke testing roles, but here is a simplified overview of different types of tester:

- **Functionality tester** – Tests the game from the player's perspective, often following testplans to cover the game feature by feature.
- **Embedded tester** – Tests individual pieces of work as they are completed by their assigned team. They may support a content department (e.g., audio) or a feature set (e.g., weapons).
- **Test automation engineer** – Writes automated scripts to test the game overnight. This role often crosses over with the more-established SDET (Software Development Engineer In Test) role from the software industry, and they will often have some experience in scripting or code.
- **Compatibility ("Compat") tester** – Checks the game on different hardware configurations looking for any issues unique to specific graphics cards, low-spec machines, or different mobile devices. Compat testing is essential for PC and mobile, as end user devices can vary enormously.
- **Certification tester** – Tests the game according to the criteria of their assigned publisher or platform. These criteria will cover loading times, save/load functionality, social features, and so on. They will often only spend a few days on each game, but if the game does not meet the criteria it will be rejected, and reapplying can be a costly affair.

Production and QA teams work together extremely closely throughout game projects. Production must ensure that the QA teams always have up-to-date information on intended game features so they can plan effective coverage.

Both teams will also collaborate on the bug-reporting systems, terminology, and communication standards, ensuring that the QA team have an effective pipeline for communicating issues to developers they may never meet.

RELEASE MANAGEMENT

A release manager's job is to ensure timely and smooth releases, overseeing the coordination, quality, and management of game launches. Throughout the project they will monitor progress, manage risks, and adjust strategies to meet release deadlines, collaborating with the development team, QA, and production. They are often the point of contact for external publishing, liaising with companies such as Microsoft, PlayStation, and Nintendo to organize a game's testing and release. They will be familiar with release platforms and requirements, and will advise the teams on how to include all the necessary platform information and metadata. Some release managers are based in publisher offices, but any large team with regular releases will generally hire a release manager to own the pipeline.

Production teams will need to consult with release managers ahead of any planned releases and ensure they know the technical requirements for submission.

LOCALIZATION (AKA "LOC")

If you want to ship your game in languages other than your own, you will need a localization team to translate your text, dialogue, and graphics. Some studios/publishers will have their own loc teams to handle all of their projects, while others will outsource their translation work to loc-specific companies.

The roles involved with localization generally include the following:

- **Translator** – Translates your content, string by string, and sends it back to you through their loc database. They will be qualified in your source language and at least one target language.
- **Loc tester (LQA)** – Tests the functionality of the loc and language systems and verifies that all the translations are correct and appropriate in-game.

- **Loc dialogue engineer** – Casts, records, and edits localized dialogue.
- **Loc voice actor** – Records localized dialogue lines. If you have a famous actor in your cast, then there is likely a popular actor in your loc language to portray them.
- **Loc project manager (LPM)** – Coordinates the translation, LQA, and loc dialogue teams to ensure your content is localized correctly and returned to you on schedule. They will be your point of contact on the loc team.
- **Loc engineer** – Sets up and manages the loc team's software (e.g., *memoQ*). They will look for opportunities to improve pipelines by directly connecting to a developer's string database, source control, and bug tracking software.
- **Cultural advisors** – These people will review your game and highlight any cultural content that may complicate your international release (e.g., music, religious iconography, contested map boundaries, etc.).

Usually one member of the internal production team will be assigned to handle the loc pipeline and be the point of contact both internally and externally. They will need to brief the loc team, work with them on the schedule, and ensure the translation pipelines run smoothly. They will also need to administrate the bugs found by the LQA team.

DEVOPS

Short for "Development Operations," the DevOps team's priority is to ensure development processes and pipelines are maintained and improved over time, so the wider development team can always keep working and becomes more and more efficient over time. This team will manage to build server infrastructure, set up content integration systems, and fix bugs in development software. They will often collaborate with the Tools, Tech Art, Tech Animation, and Tech Design teams to deploy quality-of-life improvements to the wider team.

A DevOps producer's job is to gather requests from developers, manage priorities, and workloads, and support the team in general. The DevOps team should have no development responsibilities on the game content itself, as this would detract from their DevOps work, and the investment in the wider team's longevity will grind to a halt.

LIVEOPS

LiveOps is generally a multidiscipline team which is designed to respond to the players and wider community. They will gather gameplay metrics, parse through social media, and conduct surveys to stay in touch with player sentiment, and then convert this into short-term development plans to keep their player base engaged. LiveOps content can range from quick-turnaround bug fixes, to in-game messaging, to whole content packages and scheduled events.

Common staff members of a LiveOps team include the following:

- **Data analysts** – Handle the analysis and presentation of the swathes of usage data produced by the game, with the aim of informing practical development decisions.
- **Live QA testers** – Test in accordance with the priorities of the LiveOps team, reproducing community-reported bugs and routing them appropriately through the QA and development teams to get a fixed arrangement.
- **Live developers** – Create bug fixes, update text and visual designs in response to the LiveOps team's needs. This group may include dedicated programmers, designers, or artists.

Generally there will be a dedicated live producer who coordinates the information coming from the various parts of the LiveOps team into a clear picture for the game directors. This will be used to identify development priorities to support the live product, such as hotfixes, patches, and content updates.

LEGAL

Legal teams exist to protect the company from potential legal action such as lawsuits, cease and desist letters, and claims of copyright infringement. They are particularly useful if you are looking to involve external brands or intellectual properties in your game (e.g., a soda can, a character skin, a music track, etc.) and can provide guidance on negotiation and licensing. They will also be your first consultants in case you feel it necessary to take action to protect your own intellectual property from copyright infringement or unfair usage. Small companies will have external legal consultants, whereas larger companies and publishers will have their own internal legal frameworks focused on a specific pipeline.

HR

Most game studios will have some form of human resources (HR) department. This team will generally start as a single person and will scale in size along with the studio. HR personnel manage the relationship between a company and its employees, and will be trained in the legal obligations a company has toward its employees and the mechanisms available to both employee and employer for managing each other. HR teams will often oversee various aspects of studio life and may also be involved in recruitment, onboarding, and performance review processes.

IT AND OPS

If you make video games, then you're going to need a computer. Maybe two. Any more than that and you should probably put someone in charge of IT. Joking aside, the hardware needs of a game studio scale very quickly, requiring development machines, test kits, servers, consoles, and more. You may also have a team with hundreds of different accounts on dozens of different software packages, all of which need managing. A game development team very quickly finds themselves needing an IT department to procure and update hardware, to manage software licenses, and to provide troubleshooting and IT support to the teams.

The IT department will also be responsible for digital security needs, managing the antivirus, firewalls, and VPNs that keep your source code safe from hackers and data thieves. They may also conduct exercises to test your security, such as false phishing scams and "penetration testing," which is when you pay someone to hack your company, then tell you how they managed it. The IT department is one of many which make up the wider group known as "Ops" (Operations), which will also include any team members with office-specific responsibilities, such as office managers, receptionists, and catering (generally reserved for very large studios).

PUBLISHERS

Publishers are one of the major business mechanisms that make the world of video games into an industry, and are the connection between creative development studios and the revenue of the paying market. The goal of a publisher is generally to make profit, and grow their brand which will usually favor certain genres of game. For example, the label Devolver Digital specializes in more off-beat and unusual indie games, the Fellow Traveller label is purely focused on intimate narrative games, and the giant Nintendo maintains a family-friendly brand across all its titles. Many publishers started off as development studios; Frontier Developments was a development studio for 25 years before they started offering publishing contracts to external developers in 2019.

There are many advantages of developing alongside a publisher, as they can take ownership of many complex pipelines. Services offered by publishers may include:

- Funding
- Development support
- QA support
- Localization
- Release management
- HR support
- Marketing
- Event planning
- Community management
- Permission to use their IP in your game

Generally a publisher will be approached by a group of developers with a pitch for a game, requesting funding in return for an agreed split of the profits. These pitches will need to be in alignment with the publishers goals in order to be successful; it will need to align with their brand (i.e., don't pitch a demonic gore-fest to Nintendo), it will need a viable market identified, and your team will need to look reliable enough to build it. I strongly recommend Brian Upton's GDC talk entitled "30 Things I Hate About Your Game Pitch," in which he fashions his personal experience of hearing hundreds of pitches into actionable advice.

Publisher stakeholders will generally only have a few points of contact in the development team, usually the creative director, executive producer, and head brand officer. The production team will need to ensure that the goals of the publisher are kept in focus throughout development, that content will be available to review at the requested times, and that the project is being tracked in a way to easily provide the metrics that will give the publisher confidence in the team's progress.

BRAND, MARKETING, AND COMMUNITY MANAGEMENT

The brand, marketing, and community departments will collaborate closely to manage the various relationships between the development studios and the public. While your developers can build the best game in the world, you will need experts in these positions to convince players to *buy* it:

- **Marketing manager** – Oversees the creation of marketing content to build hype for upcoming releases, such as trailers, articles, interviews, and social media campaigns. They may request content from the development teams and will likely be supported by a marketing artist.
- **Brand manager** – Owns the presentation of the game brand, and will coordinate with the design, marketing, and community teams to ensure that both the game and company's brands are represented consistently and are protected from damaging sentiment.
- **Community manager** – Act as the point of contact for the players. They are usually the ones communicating to the players when there are content updates and events or whenever the studio wishes to send a message to their community.

You should ensure that any marketing, brand, and community managers on your team receive adequate public relations (PR) training, as the public-facing environment can be complex, emotional, and dynamic. If you are more interested in the marketing side of development I can recommend visiting Chris Zukowski's website howtomarketagame.com, which contains courses and advice covering communication, store management, and data analysis.

GRACE CARROLL, LEAD COMMUNITY MANAGER

Community management is a job that differs in scope from studio to studio – it can include video creation, live streaming, event management, and more – but ultimately does come down to (as it says in the name) managing your community. The lovely and unique thing about community management specifically in the videogame industry is that unlike other industries, you are not just selling your audience a product – you are instead facilitating a conversation.

This conversation is two-way. Sometimes you will be sharing information from the studio – this could be patch notes, release date, road maps – and sometimes, you will be bringing feedback and suggestions from the players back to your developers. The most important part of this is to close the loop – you want players to feel heard and invested in your game, particularly in such a saturated market, and so you need to ensure that their feedback is valued. This could be as simple as replying to the original post and thanking them, crediting the particular user in patch notes once the issue is fixed or using public feedback boards such as Nolt or Trello to allow users to track the progress of the issue.

And of course, managing sentiment is always a vital part of the job. The way I like to think of this is as currency in a bank account: it's important to build up positive sentiment amongst players so that when you have to communicate a decision that they won't like – and you inevitably will – you are not going into the red. There is an understanding from them. This is the purpose of a lot of community management work that can seem frivolous from the outside – if you are chatting on streams, hanging out on discussion boards and making funny memes, then not only are you building up the positive sentiment, but it also means that the community don't only hear from you when there's a problem. You are not simply a bearer of bad news – you are a member of the community yourself, and this is vital.

Finally, though, it's also important to retain control of the dynamic. While you're in a conversation, the players cannot dictate the limits of the conversation – you are in control. This is not an equal partnership and you need to know when to step back and allow something to be final instead of being drawn into an argument on their level.

Of course, there's much more to community management than this – but these are the basics, and hopefully allow you a strong understanding to build on!

THE PLAYERS

Of course, we cannot forget the largest group involved in video games: the players. The reason we do all this. They can be the best thing and the worst thing about developing games.

When the times are good the players are the most incredible thing; when we launched *Alien: Isolation* we were glued to the Twitch streams watching our players getting terrified by our game, and it was absolutely joyous. Of course, when things go wrong, player sentiment can be absolutely merciless; the loudest criticisms will be the pettiest, most hurtful things they can say about your game and team. Your community manager will be the direct point of contact for the players, but the whole team should be working to enable a good relationship to be established.

Producers will rarely have direct contact with players, but they should do their best to stay aware of player sentiment. A good producer should be able to consider the game from the perspective of a player and advocate for the player's experience throughout development. Often it is an executive producer that makes the final decision on whether the game is good enough for the player, and while this might not be your role (yet) you should still be keeping the player in mind throughout.

REFERENCES

1. Johns R. 7 best programming languages for game development in 2024 [Internet]. Hackr.io. [cited 2024 Sep 10]. Available from: https://hackr.io/blog/best-programming-language-for-games
2. GlobalGameJam KG. 2009 Global Game Jam Keynote [Internet]. Youtube.com. [cited 2024 Sep 10]. Available from: https://youtu.be/aW6vgW8wc6c?si=f3gEpIjzziKU8djg

Assessing the needs
Types of game

3

Every game project is different, but there are some key aspects you can analyze to start building expectations of what your project will need to accomplish, and how you will need to run it. This chapter will explore some of the factors that will define the project you will need to architect.

GENRE

To illustrate how game needs can differ between genres, let's compare the following two games:

1. *Super Meat Boy* – A small, 2D platformer indie game
2. *The Last of Us* – A large, cinematic narrative game.

Super Meat Boy

A 2D platformer game like *Super Meat Boy* does not need to support a 3D art pipeline, has no multiplayer elements, contains hardly any written dialogue and only three words of voice-over. The game was made by two designers, who also handled the art and engineering, and a soundtrack composer. The team then had to work with some small external teams for publishing needs such as localization, testing, and uploading to Xbox Live Arcade. According to MobyGames, the credits of *Super Meat Boy* include 96 people, 48 of whom were special thanks.[1] The only "Producer" involved was on behalf of Xbox Live Arcade's publishing team.

DOI: 10.1201/9781003519065-3

The Last of Us

In contrast, to make a blockbuster "triple-AAA" narrative game like *The Last of Us*, you will need a very large development team. The fidelity of the art will require a lot of artists, and the complexity of the monsters and depth of character emotions will require a lot of animators and technical animators. The large number of gameplay mechanics and levels suggests that a lot of designers and engineers will be required. The game also has voice-over for most characters, so all these lines will need to be written by writers, recorded by actors, and edited by dialogue engineers. All the other sounds in the game needed for the creatures, weapons, and environments will need to be created and implemented by a team of sound designers and audio programmers. The game will then need extensive testing by a large team of QA testers, many of whom will be in external studios. The sheer number of assets required to construct this game will likely need more people that the studio employs, so some will have to be outsourced to keep up the pace. All of these people and needs will need to be coordinated by a team of producers, each with a dedicated set of responsibilities, reporting their pipeline's status and issues to a team of directors so the project can be steered accordingly. The large scale of this game also creates a great cost and financial risk, so the team will employ many marketing staff to increase the game's chance of commercial success and ensure that the product makes money overall. All in all, MobyGames cites 1,338 people in the credits of *The Last of Us*, including multiple different publisher departments, as well as over a dozen outsourced companies.[2]

   I'm not going to list out all the genres of video games because there are too many, they evolve too quickly, and it never covers everything. Wikipedia has an extensive run-down,[3] but to me it still feels incomplete. Where, for example, would you put Thatgamecompany's *Flower* in which you play the wind rushing through fields and valleys? The important takeaway for a producer is to be ready to adjust your approach each time you work on a different genre.

PLATFORM

There are many different game platforms you could be developing for, and each one comes with their own considerations for technology, testing, audience, and game trends.

Console

You may be developing for an established game console, such as the latest Xbox, Playstation, or Nintendo. You will need to ensure you have enough of the target hardware or your team, and programmers and QA may also request special "development kits" from the manufacturer, which enable additional features, such as rapid-mass deployment, debug configurations, and recording of performance data. You will also have to abide by the manufacturers' submission guidelines; all console manufacturers have strict submission guidelines to prevent users having a bad experience on their platform. To release the game, you will need to submit through the manufacturers' submissions pipeline (which comes with a cost) and they will check your game against their guidelines. It will need to pass their checks before it can go out onto the store for that console. These checks range from performance guidelines (e.g., minimum FPS and load screen times) to the inclusion of entire features and content sets (e.g., Xbox achievements). It is worth studying these requirements early in development so you can plan for them.

PC

Instead of consoles, you may instead be developing for Windows PC, and perhaps releasing on Steam, Epic Store, or Windows Store. In place of development kits you will need plenty of high-power computers. If your game is multiplayer, many of your team members will need two PCs that they can run simultaneously. Submission criteria on PC is generally less controlled than the console pipelines, so you will have to define your own guidelines for minimum performance levels. Player hardware can vary wildly, and you will want to specify a minimum-supported configuration (e.g., processor speed, GPU, memory, etc.). To sustain this quality bar you will need a team of compliance testers who can test the game on as many configurations of common hardware as possible, so that you can find out ahead of time if your game has a problem with a certain chip-set, motherboard, or graphics driver. Customer support for PC games can get extremely technical, so you should be prepared to deal with customers complaining about issues that may only affect people with a certain hardware configuration.

Mobile

In recent years, the mobile game industry has grown explosively, and now rivals the size and revenue of the PC and console industries that have thus far dominated the market, and they need producers too. A project on a mobile game is going to differ greatly from your traditional console game in many ways. Most obviously, it will be a shorter cycle from development to release; a console game can take many years, whereas mobile game studios will often try to get a new title through the door in three to six months. However, for most mobile games this is not the end of development by any means, and many will run a "soft launch" in which they release their game on the store in a select number of regions with minimal marketing. After soft launch, the data side of mobile development gets involved, with the game designers working with internal data teams and analysts to try and understand their players behavior to the smallest detail; What time of day do they play? How long do they play for? What in-game events cause players to stop? Much of this relates to how players interact with a mobile game; rather than sit down in an evening for several hours like with a console game, many mobile games will be played for 5–10 min at a time, often on public transport, at the coffee machine, or – it must be said – on the toilet. Playing a mobile game is a momentary habit, rather than a time-consuming hobby. The user data gathered allows the design teams to continually adjust how the game works to maximize player retention and train their habits toward the part of the app that makes the money. Mobile games will often localize their games into as many languages as possible, which gives their app as much chance to find a successful market as possible; the Asia-Pacific region has colossal mobile game markets,[4] and most gaming in Africa is on mobile.[5] Being a producer on a mobile game will feel very different to working on a console or PC game, in that your focus will be less polishing a single title, and more about the rock-solid processes that produce a game, gather measurable data on everything about it, and inform the decisions that optimize the game's market performance on the fly.

A note on VR development

A VR headset (e.g., Meta Quest 3, Apple Vision Pro, etc.) is effectively a console, so all the rules of console development still apply, but you should also expect the need for more office space per person, as they will need the physical space you are developing for. If your VR game is being run on a PC, then expect all the compatibility challenges of PC development to need addressing as well.

Producers will need to study the platform they are shipping for, and learn the different challenges they will present, allowing the producer to be vigilant for potential pitfalls later on in the project.

STAKEHOLDERS

The question here is "who is your team working for?" A stakeholder is a group or individual that has decision-making authority over your project, and they will rely on the production team to keep them informed of progress and ensure they are made aware of problems at their level. Here are some stakeholder examples and how the relationship with each one can shape development.

Publisher

Most commercial games have some form of publisher agreement. The publisher effectively employs the development studio to make a game and provides the funding ahead of development. This will generally be delivered in chunks throughout the project, as the team completes the agreed milestones. The publisher will also have their own goals for the project, which could relate to the number of sales, the overall narrative, or opportunities for merchandise. Sometimes the IP will be owned by the publisher, and other times by the developer, depending on the agreement at the beginning of the project. Most large publishers also have their own localization, QA, marketing, and release pipelines in place and made available to the developer. If the publisher is a console manufacturer, then they may insist that the developer set up their game to demonstrate a new feature, such as the touch-pad on a PlayStation 5 dual-sense controller, or the hand-tracking in VR.

Client

Many game studios and work-for-hire businesses focus entirely on contracted games. In these cases, the client – such as a movie publisher – will reach out to the studio with a brief for a game they want created, such as a tie-in game for their movie release. In many ways this will be a similar project to the publisher arrangement, with a pre-agreed milestone schedule, incremental payments, and the need to understand the goals of the client. It is very unlikely that your studio will retain any IP rights after such a project. Although you are working to meet the client's goals, it will also be crucial to know your own business goals (e.g., financial growth, brand-building, marketing strategy, etc.) and to ensure that these are not jeopardized in service of the client. The projects will require mindful steering to achieve this balance throughout.

Co-development ("Co-dev")

Large game studios will often contract a "co-dev" studio to handle a certain part of their game. That co-dev studio may be an external company, or they could be a dedicated entity within the company. For example, Ubisoft Reflections is a studio in England that does most of the vehicle development for Ubisoft games that have driving elements. In a role such as this you will likely be running a fairly repetitive pipeline; the goal of a co-dev studio is to be an efficient resource for responding to requests. Using vehicles as an example, you can expect your partner studios to request a number of vehicles per game/release, each with a brief and a deadline. Your team will then process the requests and provide the assets in the requested timeline. A producer in a co-dev studio will have to receive these requests, get all brief questions answered, provide quotes, set up agreements for timelines and deliverables, and manage their delivery. A good producer should also be looking out for any ways in which the repeated processes can be improved so the company can keep improving its efficiency. These changes may be technological improvements, project processes, or improved communication standards and pipelines. Given that co-dev is often a repeated pipeline, all process improvements are high-value investments over time.

Yourselves

Maybe you have none of these stakeholders, instead you are living the indie dream, making a game just for yourselves and whatever players you can find. If you're making the game as a hobby, or as an artistic project, and there is no financial reliance on the game's success, then you can run the project with no real structure at all. However, if you have a team, any investors, or ambitions for business growth, then it will be down to you as the producer to help your team decide what your own goals will be, how you judge your own success, and how you will know that you are on track for your own aspirations. These goals may relate to sales, profit, budget endurance, investor uptake, signing a technology deal, winning awards, and more. Or maybe you're not thinking about any of this, and you just want the world to rejoice in terrorizing a village as a horrible goose. (Have I told you I love video games?)

RELEASE/MONETIZATION FORMAT

Not every game is sold in the same way. Game developers have forever experimented with how they get their products in front of players, and how they can make the best return from the transactions and habits involved. Here are the main methods being used today by game developers, and how you can expect them to impact a producer's role during the project.

"Boxed product"

This is the classic routine where you make the game, and then sell it directly to players for a price. As per the name, this used to involve a physical cartridge or disc, and then the box and packaging to go with it, whereas now most games are digital download only. The routine is fairly similar, with a preproduction, production, and finaling stage. Key differences in the digital age are the largely eliminated costs and logistics of shipping, but also the promise of postlaunch online support. Most games development teams will now create a "Release build" which is used for certification, and will be the first build uploaded to the chosen store (e.g., Steam, Xbox, PlayStation Network, etc.), but the team will continue to fix bugs on a separate "Day 1 patch" build, which will be made available to download on release day. This allows development teams more bug-fixing time right up to the end of development. Generally teams will also support the game after launch with patches and fixes, depending on consumer issues.

DLC (downloadable content)

Many developers of "Boxed product" games will release DLC after the release of the main game. This can come in the form of additional playable missions, maps, characters, or cosmetics for the characters and weapons. Some smaller DLC packs may be released for free which keeps the players invested in the game long after launch, with the larger DLC packs being released for payment. The first batch of DLC content is usually planned alongside the main project and will be worked into a postlaunch plan. Sometimes DLC will be scheduled for release on the same day as the main game, and this will have been developed alongside the main game content.

Subscription

A few games run a subscription-based access model, with the players paying a monthly fee for access to the game world. These have mostly been titles in the MMORPG genre, such as Blizzard's *World of Warcraft,* or CCP's *EVE Online.* A subscription model works for games that are designed to be a persistent world with a long-term player presence and commitment and allows new players to try the game out for a low initial cost, after which they can choose to back out or pay to stay. *EVE Online* actually manifests the subscription time as objects in the game world, which can be bought and traded between players (and destroyed by clumsy pirates[6]), usually for a very high in-game price.

Free-to-play (aka "freemium")

Quite a recent style of release and monetization, so-called "free-to-play" games, gives players access to their game with no payment up front, in order to grow their player-base as quickly as possible (the business term for this is "loss-leading"). Developers will design the games to form habits for the player, and then offer incentives to spend money within those habits. These transactions have become known as "micro-transactions," as they are usually much smaller than the price of a game but, as they build up over a long time, can be extremely lucrative for a developer. A good example of microtransactions can be seen in Riot Games' *League of Legends*, which allows players to pay to add a playable character to their player roster, which would otherwise be rotated out of play each week. Other examples include paying to speed up a game mechanic (e.g., crop growth in Zynga's *Farmville*), or paying for additional costumes for a character (e.g., in miHoYo's *Genshin Impact*). Some developers also incorporate adverts into free-to-play games and generate revenue from these. They also sometimes pair this with an available microtransaction to skip the adverts (e.g., Kolibri's *Idle Miner Tycoon*). A key element of many of these strategies is the creation of an "in-game currency" (e.g., Riot Points in *League of Legends*) which acts as a proxy between the player's real life wallet and the in-game content; this currency can be slowly earned through grinding gameplay, or instantly purchased by the player from the in-game store using real money. This separation from real money means the game economy can be more easily managed, and arguably it makes the user more willing to complete the microtransaction, as it feels less like spending "real money." Free-to-play game producers will need a good understanding of their game's monetization structure, as this will inform the priorities, requirements, and constraints of feature development.

Arcade video game

Yes, they still exist! Developing these games is essentially the same as creating a "boxed-product" style game, but instead of selling the game directly to players, the studio/publisher will rent out the arcade machines to venues, who get to keep all the money in the machine and benefit from the game attracting customers to their premises, who may in turn spend more money on food and drink.

REFERENCES

1. Super Meat Boy [Internet]. MobyGames. [cited 2024 Sep 10]. Available from: https://www.mobygames.com/game/48877/super-meat-boy/
2. The Last of Us [Internet]. MobyGames. [cited 2024 Sep 10]. Available from: https://www.mobygames.com/game/60922/the-last-of-us/
3. Wikipedia contributors. List of video game genres [Internet]. Wikipedia, The Free Encyclopedia. 2024. Available from: https://wikipedia.org/w/index. php?title=List_of_video_game_genres&oldid=1235402589
4. Rousseau J. Global Data: Asia-Pacific region made up 64% of mobile gaming revenue in 2023 [Internet]. GamesIndustry.biz. 2024 [cited 2024 Sep 10]. Available from: https://www.gamesindustry.biz/global-data-asia-pacific-region-made-up-64-of-mobile-gaming-revenue-in-2023
5. Video Games – Africa [Internet]. Statista. [cited 2024 Sep 10]. Available from: https://www.statista.com/outlook/dmo/digital-media/video-games/africa
6. Drain B. EVE player destroys over $1000 worth of game time [Internet]. Engadget. 2010 [cited 2024 Sep 10]. Available from: https://www.engadget. com/2010-08-08-eve-player-destroys-over-1000-worth-of-game-time.html

Building a schedule
Project phases

4

While every game project is unique, there are some terms that have become very common language and are essential knowledge for a game producer. What follows is a high-level overview of the standard phases of a project, and the responsibilities you can expect as a producer during each one, with the first being the project kick-off.

KICK-OFF (WHAT ARE WE MAKING?)

This is the moment when one or more people commit to making a game. For an indie game this could simply be two friends meeting up in a coffee shop and saying "Ok, so we're going to make a game about a tiny lumberjack. Where do we start?" However, established development studios and publishers will have a formal process in which a contract is discussed, defined, and signed. This contract will stipulate the basic concept (e.g., a co-op fantasy role-playing game), the budget, a high-level schedule, key stakeholders, revenue split, and any other constraints such as target platforms and IP rights. The production team will gather information to aid the pitching and contract signing, with the executive producer likely providing one of the closing signatures.

CONCEPTING (FIND THE QUESTIONS)

Project concepting is the short period where the team expands the initial game concept into a huge list of ideas, questions, and goals that will lead toward

DOI: 10.1201/9781003519065-4

the brief being satisfied. The key goal of project concepting is to identify the questions that will need answering ahead of the production phase, which will effectively create the plan for preproduction, where the questions will actually be answered.

Here are some questions that might be identified during this time:

- What is our gameplay loop?
- What are the key beats of the story?
- What locations will we need to construct?
- What gameplay mechanics need designing?
- What systems will we need to build?
- What team members do we need to recruit?
- What outsourcers and services will we need?

This will vary from project to project, but the goal of identifying questions remains the same.

PREPRODUCTION (ANSWER THE QUESTIONS)

In preproduction your team should be answering the questions gathered during concepting. Here are some common methods the various teams will use to do this:

- **Competitive analysis** – Looking at other games to understand current trends in style, gameplay, and design heuristics
- **Create style guides** – These core documents will help keep the art and audio consistent throughout the project.
- **Build prototypes** – Programmers, designers, artists, and sound designers will all need to prove out the systems they think they will need to power the game.
- **Prove out technical pipelines** – The teams should ensure that they can author and submit assets correctly into the game through the desired tools and source control pipelines.
- **Purchase code/asset libraries** – There will likely be various libraries that the team identifies for purchase which save a lot of development time early on.

- **Identify outsourcing needs** – All the teams should identify where outsourcing can save them time or fill key skill gaps.
- **Plan excursions** – Some teams may need to plan trips, such as on-location research and reference gathering, or audio field recordings.
- **Draft up schedules and budgets** – The team should be starting to reckon with how much money they each have, and how far it will stretch.

Preproduction is arguably the most important phase in the whole project, as it is the last opportunity to define your direction before you ramp up the size of the team, and accelerate the work. If you accelerate the team without a clear direction, you will burn through time and money without making any progress toward your goal, so it is often better to take the extra time and ensure all the key development questions are answered.

PRODUCTION (MAKE THE GAME)

Production is when you stop brainstorming, settle on a plan, and get on with it. You've drawn up all your plans, listed up all your features, you've got a schedule ahead of you that may stretch on for years, and somewhere at the end of it there is a great new video game waiting to exist. The designers will be blocking out levels and fleshing out the mechanics, artists will be building assets, programmers will be constructing the systems, and so on. The production phase is like an assembly line, and it's the production team's job to keep that assembly line running for as long as is needed; it is rare for a nonmobile game to be built in less than two years, and very common for larger games to take four years or more for completion, with production being the longest phase.

The producer's main responsibilities will include tracking the tasks, measuring and reporting on progress, and flagging up potential risks. Also, if your team has a problem, it is your job to see that it is resolved quickly and to put processes in place to prevent it from recurring. Producers should also be keeping tabs on the health and mood of the team; production is a long haul and you will need to make sure your team can sustain their output without getting burned out.

The production phase nears its end when the majority of features and content have been completed, and then you are ready to proceed to alpha.

ALPHA (POLISH IT)

By the time you reach alpha you should effectively have a finished game, and now is the time to polish it and start preparing it for release. During alpha the team will be looking at artistic polish, audio polish, and final game balancing, much of which will come from feedback from leads, directors, publishers, and even the public; many studios invite a number of players to participate in a "closed alpha" in which they sign a nondisclosure agreement (NDA), are given a license, and play the game, providing feedback en masse to the community team. Producers should note that the alpha phase can be quite challenging for the team emotionally, because it means time is running out, and the team will have to start turning down opportunities. The producers should regularly provide the team with a clear view of their remaining time and agency, so they can prioritize their best remaining ideas.

Alpha is also when any text, voice, and images for translation should be sent to the localization team so they can begin the huge task of recreating your game's content in different languages. There will likely be some text polish and vocal pickups still to come, which will need to be sent along later. Meanwhile, the QA team will be running meticulous sweeps of the entire game, testing every feature, every map, and every line of dialogue to verify that the whole game is functioning as the developers intended. This will be generating a huge list of bugs for the team to work through in the beta phase.

BETA (TEST IT)

The time for polish is over. This is the last stage before you wrap up the game and release it. By the time you reach beta, the QA team should have verified that all the major features of your game are working as intended, and they will now be trying to break the game any way they can. During this time hundreds and maybe even thousands of bugs will be created, prioritized, fixed, and waived. The creative teams will mostly be off the project, and anyone remaining should be focused purely on fixing the bugs that come in. Producers will need to support the bug pipeline, ensuring the QA teams have regular builds, checking that everyone is aware of the bugs assigned to them, and chasing whoever needs chasing to make sure no bugs get stuck in the pipeline. Producers are often the ones prioritizing the reported bugs, balancing the impact on the player with the risk of the fix, trying to ensure the teams' limited bug-fixing time is spent in the best way possible. Additionally, the last of the text and voice content should now be locked and sent to the localization team for translation.

Some games also run closed/open beta periods with some of the keener members of the public. This is not so much about generating bugs (your QA teams should be handling that) but helping to prioritize them, as the ongoing feedback from the players will highlight which issues they are most concerned about. Some of these issues will be about game balancing, and the design team may have opportunities to fix a few numeric game elements to improve the way the game plays (e.g., weapon damage values, ammo quantities, cool-down timers on abilities, etc.). This feedback will generally be gathered and reported by your community managers, but production may have to help convey the information to the design and QA teams.

When the release approaches, the production and QA teams will identify a build that is good enough quality to release, and they will prepare this build for the last stage: finaling.

FINALING (WRAP IT UP)

Once a release build has been identified, you are now in the finaling stage. From this point, if nothing goes wrong, you now have the game that will be sent out to a world of players to enjoy. Your QA team's testing will now be purely focused on the specific criteria for your release platform. For example, if you are releasing on a PlayStation console, then you will test against the latest PlayStation release criteria, so that their own team will find no problems, which could delay the release and cost extra money.

Once your QA team signs off the build, you then hand it over to the release manager/team. They will run their checks on the build, and upload it to the platform, ready to be enabled on release day. We're almost there…

RELEASE (SHIP IT)

With your final checks complete, it's time to ship! This used to mean sending packaged games to high-street stores to be ready for release day, but in the world of digital games it simply means "turning it on" in that platform's online store. Now players will be able to purchase it, download it, and start playing your game. Some of those players may have already preordered and predownloaded the game ahead of release day, depending on the release strategy.

To coincide with the release, the marketing teams will be flooding all the social media and store channels with content to celebrate and publicize the launch, so that everyone knows you've arrived. If you provided any early builds to reviewers, they will now publish their reviews to various websites, magazines, and video channels. Meanwhile, the community and QA teams will all be on high-alert, watching the forums and social media channels for any problems that players are having getting access to the game. The producers will be supporting these teams on gathering issues and preparing the live teams to work on hot-fixes. They will also arrange the project postmortem and, of course, the wrap party!

Congratulations! You've shipped the game! It's over...

POST-RELEASE CONTENT (RETAIN THE PLAYERS)

...well, to be honest it's never really over. In the days before the internet, shipping the game generally meant the end of the work on it, and you would set the team to work on the next one. Over time some games would start to do mission packs, map packs and expansions, but these would be another disc entirely. I remember buying additional levels for ID Software's *Quake,* and extra missions for Westwood Studios' *Command and Conquer: Red Alert.* Nowadays this is routine; nearly every game release will have some kind of follow-up or DLC, ranging from bug-fixing patches, to additional missions and levels, to new multiplayer characters, to cosmetic items for purchase and to new seasonal events for the community.

For live games (including most mobile titles) the day of release is only the beginning; as the players arrive and start to explore the game, the shape of the experience starts to truly form for the first time, and the teams will be watching all the analytics, forums, and social media to figure out all the tweaks to keep the momentum going, and to find that sweet spot where the players will never get bored of your game.

Some producers will be working with these live teams on the bug-fixing and patches, helping to identify priorities, keep communication slick and efficient, and help to keep the community supported by the development team. Others may have moved on to the next piece of DLC and will be back in preproduction with the development team on something new.

RECAP

As a summary for this section, I'm simply going to list the project phases and the purpose of each, as you will likely need to teach this to your teams and developers many times during your career:

- **Kick-off:** What are we making?
- **Concepting:** Find the questions
- **Pre-production:** Answer the questions
- **Production:** Make the game
- **Alpha:** Polish it
- **Beta:** Test it
- **Finaling:** Wrap it up
- **Release:** Ship it
- **Post-release content:** Retain the players

Planning the work

5

Project components

While every game project is different, the job of the producer will still be to help their team gather their ideas and put them together into a viable project. This chapter is dedicated to exploring the different parts of a project, and how those parts can vary from studio to studio, team to team, and game to game. We'll look at how games themselves can vary by genre, platform, and monetization style, take a tour through the standard phases of a project, and finally focus on some key production areas, such as budgets, outsourcing, and version control.

WHAT IS A MILESTONE ANYWAY?

In short, a milestone is the date by which the bosses want some important stuff done. These milestones may also define the payment schedule from publisher to developer. An example of an initial project schedule for a medium-sized game (70-ish developers at peak) could look like this:

- 0 months – Project kick-off – $500,000 paid
- 6 months – Playable prototype – $2,500,000 paid
- 12 months – Vertical Slice – $15,000,000 paid
- 30 months – Alpha – $5,000,000 paid
- 36 months – Release – $1,500,000 paid

If the deliverable is met, the publisher will pay the money to fund the next stage of development. Each publisher will likely have their own preferred

DOI: 10.1201/9781003519065-5

cadence for milestones; they could be years apart, or monthly. It depends on the developer/publisher relationship. On the approach to each milestone the specific *deliverables* will be discussed and communicated to the team. These may be prototypes, features, or areas of content. An individual milestone breakdown may look like this:

Milestone 5 – due 25th June

Deliverables:

- Character 1 – Concept/3D model/animation/audio complete
- Character 2 – Concept/3D model complete
- Characters 3/4/5 – Concept art complete
- Level 1 – Env art/lighting/audio complete
- Level 2 – Env art complete
- Level 3/4/5 – Env art blockout playable
- Chapter system – Implementation complete
- Item crafting – Prototype playable

When these deliverables are presented, they should be accompanied by a presentation of *definitions*. This is to ensure that the stakeholders and the development team all have the same understanding of the requirements. Here is a possible example (will vary by game and studio):

Definition – "env art complete"

- All buildings, vehicles, and furniture are final
- All textures are final
- All VFX is final
- Sky-box is final
- Navigation mesh is generated
- Collectible item slots are placed

A producer will usually be given charge of coordinating a milestone delivery. They will need to prioritize the milestone tasks with the leads, make them visible to the team, track their progress, and give people timely reminders of the deadlines. They should also communicate if it looks like some of the deliverables will not meet the deadline, at which point the leads can prioritize again.

Delivering a large milestone usually comes with a lot of pressure, and the experience can be draining for the team, so a producer may see fit to arrange a "milestone wrap party," which would be food and drink ordered to the office, a paid meal out for the team, or some other fun activity (did you know you can hire puppies to the office?).

TASKS AND THEIR MANY FORMS

Most production jobs will include managing a database of tasks, which are used to help quantify work, measure progress and, more so these days, streamline communications on specific issues. While the leads and creatives should generally be the ones defining the tasks, the production team is responsible for building and maintaining the task-tracking pipeline and ensuring it supports all the departments.

There are many ways that tasks are tracked throughout the industry:

- **Project management software (complex)** – Large teams generally use high-powered suites such as *Jira*, *Asana*, or *Helix Plan*. These packages enable lots of data gathering, reporting, and contain advanced communication and workflow configuration features.
- **Project management software (simple)** – Smaller teams may use simpler software packages like *Trello*, *HacknPlan*, or *Slack Lists,* which have fewer features but require less overhead and are generally less intimidating for new team members.
- **Spreadsheets** – Some teams are small enough to keep their project management in shared spreadsheets. This keeps overhead low, and a producer that's good with their spreadsheets can create very intuitive task-tracking environments, but it will come with fewer features.
- **Sticky notes** – Many teams – if they are in the same location – will still use sticky notes on a wall to track their tasks. The Post-it® company has even released an app which allows a user to scan a wall of notes directly to the cloud.

In the world of project management, a lot of teams have started to use multiple different types of tasks to organize, categorize, and streamline their workflows. While each team will create their own, here are a few common example types that a new producer should be ready to discuss.

Task

Simply "a thing that needs to be done." It needs to include enough information for the developer to act upon it. Tasks are generally written by the area/feature lead with support from the producer and are usually contained within an Epic (see below).

An example task title could be: "DESIGN – Campaign – Abilities progression system – 1st Pass."

Sub-task

Sub-Tasks are very small pieces of work that will be contained within either a Task or User Story (see below), and are generally written by the developer for their own personal use, to break down the larger task above it. A *recklessly* simplified example could look like this:

- Task: "CODE – Gameplay – Implement player movement controller"
- Sub-Tasks:
  - "Set up input tracker"
  - "Configure velocity curve"
  - "Configure jump values"
  - "Test default controls"
  - "Expose parameters to UI settings controller"
  - "Expose parameters to animation engine"
  - "Test remapped controls"

User story

A term from Agile software development (more on this in Chapter 6) which is more common with live and mobile games. A User Story does not specify the exact work, but rather documents the required outcome for the user. The standard writing convention for User Stories is:

- Template: "As a [user] I want [a feature] so that I may [outcome]."
- Example: "As a *player*, I want a *menu showing my objectives* so that I may review them during a mission."

User stories are generally written by a product owner in software development, but in games this is generally done by design leads. Once written it will then be passed to a developer, who will break it down into the required Sub-Tasks to achieve the outcomes. They are usually contained within an Epic (see below).

Epic

An Epic is a container for Tasks/User Stories, and generally represents a content feature, or a system. They are used to help organize the tasks for development and are useful for tracking progress from a high level. Example Epics could be:

- **ENV – Hangar**: Contains all the design, environment art, and audio tasks for the "Hangar" level
- **SYS – Save/Load**: Contains all the design, UI, and code tasks for the save/load system
- **UNIT – Battle Tank**: Contains all the design, art, animation, code, and audio tasks for the "Battle Tank" unit.

Please note that, while the above naming convention is not a standard, it is worth ensuring you *have* naming conventions for your Tasks and Epics. Good naming conventions keep your systems readable and communicable.

Initiative

It is an increasingly common term on large projects which refers to a collection of Epics. For example, an Initiative may be a faction in a strategy game and will contain all the Epics for that faction's units, abilities, and environments. This can again help to organize the Epics and tasks on these large projects and divide up the areas of ownership between different leads and producers.

Modern tasks tend to contain a lot of information to provide context and direction for the required work. Here are some examples of commonly retained information in tasks and user stories:

- **Summary** – A concise line that explains the task, for which the team will likely have a standard naming convention (e.g., "ENV – GARAGE – Stack of car tyres – MODEL)
- **Assignee** – The person currently responsible for acting on the work
- **Estimate** – How long the task is expected to take
- **Story points** – (Only used with user stories)

- **Success criteria** – Clear guidance for acknowledging that the task is done (e.g., "3D model placed in level")
- **Category** – Some kind of categorization to help organize and measure the work. This may be used for departments (e.g., art, audio, and code), or it may be used for phases of work (e.g., concept, final, optimization, etc.)
- **Deadline** – The date/milestone by which the task is expected to be done
- **Parent** – This may be the feature/area that the task is contained within, and is used to keep work organized
- **Description** – Any supplemental information or context worth adding to that task.

It's important to remember that task-tracking is a means to an end, and it should be seen as a tool in service of a greater goal. Every element of the pipeline should be configured to help the developers achieve their creative goals in the game.

BUGS

A bug is a defect in a piece of technology. There is a myth that the name comes from insects getting caught in the punch cards of early computers, but the use of "bug" as meaning "defect" actually dates back to the 1800s.[1] Bugs are generally unforeseen outcomes of complex system development and can result in crashes, graphical glitches, or faults in the game logic which create undesirable outcomes for the player. A defect found during development will be recorded in a "bug report" by the QA team, which is then sent to the development team for bug-fixing. As development proceeds, the QA team will be assigned to cover large areas of the game and check that they are working as intended.

Testing methods

The QA team does a lot more than simply "play the game" and will use an array of methods to ensure their coverage of the game is exhaustive:

- **Testplans** – Extensive checklists covering every implemented aspect of the game; every weapon, level, character, UI button, and line of dialogue will be listed out and assigned a tester.

- **Styled playthroughs** – Testing a game with a specific player style, for example, "collect every item," "fail every test once," "use zero upgrades," and so on.
- **Destructive testing** – QA unleash their inner weirdo, and do all the strange things that players do in games to break it any way they can; grapple onto a moving bicycle, fill the spaceship with potatoes, drop a grenade just before a cutscene, and so on.
- **Automated testing** – Using purposefully scripted bots to carry out player-like behaviors many times over and over again to flag up issues.
- **Public alphas/betas** – Inviting the public to help test the game in late stages of development, with the internal QA and community teams triaging the bugs and feedback. A team of 30 testers over three years will log fewer gameplay hours than 100,000 members of the public manage in a single day.

The QA and production teams work together closely on the pipeline of finding and fixing bugs. The QA team will report back with a huge list of bugs, and the production team will need to go through them and assign priorities. This process is often called "triage," and the producer may do it alone, or they may collaborate with a development lead and a QA tester.

What's in a bug report?

Every game studio will have their own language and conventions for bug reporting which will relate to their game and team structure. However, there are some fields you can expect to see, in some form, in every game project's bug database:

- **Summary** – A short description of the bug, often following a naming convention (e.g., "LEVEL 2 – CRASH – Game crashes when completing level 2 without finding the Crystal Shield").
- **Severity (aka Class)** – How impactful the bug is to the player. Set by QA.
- **Priority** – How important the bug is to be fixed. Set by the production team or area lead.
- **Assignee** – The person currently responsible for acting on the bug.
- **Category** – The type of bug encountered (e.g., crash, visual glitch, logical error, etc.). Will differ per studio and game.
- **Game area** – The affected game area (e.g., level 2, main menu, troll character, etc.). This further helps to categorize the bugs and get them to the right developer for fixing.

- **Reporter** – The QA tester that reported the bug. The developers may contact this tester with clarifying questions.
- **Description** – A more full description than the summary, where the tester can give as much information as needed to give context to the issue.
- **Attached media** – Screenshots and videos of the issue. Some testing tools record these automatically.
- **Reproduction steps** – A clear list of instructions for triggering the issue, so anyone receiving the issue can trigger it for themselves, and test their fix. For example:
  1. – Boot game from launcher
  2. – Load Level 2 from Chapter Select screen
  3. – Follow the objectives as normal up to the cave section
  4. – Take the tunnel on the left and skip the shield hall
  5. – Go to the end of level door
  6. – Observe crash when turning handle
- **Reproduction rate** – How reliably the bug can be triggered (e.g., 3/3 attempts)
- **Expected result** – What the tester believes should be happening in that moment (e.g., "The user should be told 'You cannot progress without the crystal shield'.")

Common types of bug/error

Every new game creates new bugs, but here are some common terms used in regards to bugs in game development:

- **Assert** – The game halts and shows a debug message. These are set up by programmers to catch undesirable events in the code and will often give instructions as to who to contact.
- **Crash** – A catastrophic outcome is detected by the code (e.g., running out of memory) and the game stops entirely. When logging a crash, QA testers will generally be asked to attach a callstack – a batch of code that provides a snapshot of all the active processes at the time of the crash.
- **Softlock** – The player can no longer progress. This can be a door that doesn't open, a line of dialogue that never plays, or the player becomes trapped by a physical object.
- **De-sync** – When the players are no longer synchronized in an online game. For example, Player A may shoot and kill Player B, but Player B's game did not register the impact or the death, causing the games to go out of sync.

- **Clipping** – When part of a 3D model visibly passes through another 3D model, such as a character's arm passing through a wall
- **Physics glitch** – When an object's physics model gets confused, causing unusual behavior, such as a knocked chair bouncing around the room like a tennis ball
- **Performance** – Refers to any issues which drop the frame-rate of the game to unpleasant levels. Many studios will define a minimum acceptable FPS which if passed, requires a bug report (e.g., 60 FPS or lower).
- **Save/load** – Save data is incorrectly loaded. For example, the player's save may fail to load all of their items, their upgrades, or their progress in a mission.
- **Text/localization** – This will refer to any issues in which the wrong text is displaying, either in your main language or in localized languages.
- **Certification (aka "Cert")** – When an issue is known to violate the certification criteria of the release platform. These are usually only reported by certification testers or teams conducting their own "pre-certification" test passes.

Severity (aka "class")

This field is a way for testers to communicate how badly the encountered bug will impact the player. While not strictly an industry standard, the below ABCD class system is a commonly followed convention:

- **Severity A** – Creates an unacceptable situation for the player (e.g., crash, softlock, loss of save data, etc.) or would block the release of the game. Generally games will ship with zero severity A issues. At least, zero *known* issues…
- **Severity B** – Severely disrupts the gameplay experience such as giving the player incorrect information, forcing them to reload a save, or stacking the game against them unfairly. Generally games ship with very few severity B issues.
- **Severity C** – Visual and cosmetic issues that do not block the player, but can break immersion and make the experience feel less polished. Usually covers clipping, physics and audio issues, but there can be exceptions; I myself have logged audio bugs as severity B when they had the potential to deafen the player.
- **Severity D** – Generally these aren't really bugs, but are often design suggestions. They rarely get fixed, but are still worth reporting. Look for good ideas everywhere.

Production bug-fixing responsibilities

The producers are responsible for ensuring that the testing, reporting, and bug-fixing pipelines are all efficiently working for the whole team, which boils down to these key needs:

- QA team is informed when a feature is complete and ready for them to test.
- The schedule allocates time for testing and bug-fixing to occur.
- Test plans are agreed upon by both QA and developers.
- QA team has the necessary hardware and software for effective testing.
- Bug-tracking system is appropriately configured for all teams.
- Bug triage happens regularly.

A common trap in game development is when the team fails to protect the time required to adequately test the game to full coverage, which leads to a lot of testers and developers crunching to find and fix as much as possible, despite which there will still be more bugs in your final product than they would want. I advise all producers to treat your testing schedules as seriously as your release deadlines; it will build more sustainable practice, keep your teams healthier, and help you release a more solid game.

MIKE WEBB – AUTOMATION ENGINEER

Auto tests can be used to remove the need for QA to perform simple or repetitive tasks so that they can focus their time and effort on other areas of the project. There is usually an automation tool which is used to coordinate the running of the tests and the recording of the results. Each auto test is defined as a success criteria; if it doesn't meet the requirements by the end of the test, then it will be flagged as a failure. Other errors can be picked up as part of the auto test, even though the test itself may be successful, such as flagging missing data files or sending warnings to specific departments.

There are many categories of auto tests, some of which are listed here:

AUTOMATED BVT (BUILD VERIFICATION TESTS)

When a new version of the game is built with the latest developer code and game data, auto tests can be run against it to check the stability before it goes out to QA and other teams. Automated BVT tests include:

- *Launching the game to the title screen, then clicking through menus to load into each area of the game, confirming that it is possible to do so without major problems occurring such as crashes or the software locking up.*
- *Simple checks on major game systems to ensure they are functioning well enough that testing can be done on the latest build. For example, in a First Person Shooter, tests might include checking that weapons can fire and do damage correctly, players and enemies can heal and die, levels can be completed, etc.*

PERFORMANCE CHECKS

- *Benchmarks – Scripted camera fly-throughs of representative gameplay which record the performance and memory usage of the game over a period of time. These are run on multiple platforms and PC hardware, and analyzed to see where the performance may decrease and improvements can be made on the running of the game.*
- *Loading times – Usually done with the BVT checks, auto tests may also record how long it takes to load into every area of the game and flag to developers when it goes over a threshold.*
- *Soak tests – The auto test will load into the main menu or a specific area of the game, then sit there for a long period of time before performing other actions. These will detect issues such as memory leaks that may not occur during a normal gameplay session.*

COMPATIBILITY CHECKS

- *A PC game will usually have a large range of settings which the player can change to improve the performance or the visual quality. Auto tests can be used to loop through every single combination of these settings over multiple PCs to check that the game doesn't break at any point.*
- *More recently, even console games have graphical settings which the player can change, so auto tests may cover these as well.*

LOCALIZATION

TAMARA TIRJAK – HEAD OF LOCALIZATION AT FRONTIER DEVELOPMENTS

Let me invite you to play a game of "True or False?", where we discuss some of the (mis)conceptions around game localization.

"LOCALIZATION = TRANSLATION"

False! While translating the game from one language (the "source") into one or more new languages (the "target"), localization normally incorporates a range of additional activities, such as:

- *Internationalization: to collect and enforce development best practices to ensure that the game is "world-ready." This means things such as ensuring the fonts for all supported languages display correctly, there are no hard-coded unlocalizable strings, or that different date and time formats are supported to respect local conventions.*
- *Text pipeline development: to enable the implementation of multilingual assets in the game build.*
- *Culturalization: to ensure that the visual assets, the characters, and the story of the game are crafted with the global audience in mind. Committing cultural misappropriation or discussing sensitive geopolitical topics in a disrespectful way is a quick way to anger the masses. It can even get your game banned in certain territories. On the other hand, getting your game to positively resonate with a multicultural audience is a vital step toward global success.*
- *Multilingual voice-over: to ensure that your NPCs sound equally awesome in any language.*
- *Platform certification: to comply with the console glossary and language requirements from platform holders.*

"AS A PRODUCER, I HAVE TO FOCUS ON MAKING THE GAME. LOCALIZATION WILL TAKE CARE OF THE REST."

False! As a Producer you can fuel the success of the localization programme by ensuring two things:

Connections

Just like any other discipline in the game team, localization does not happen in isolation. They will work with Programmers on the pipeline tools, with UI on internationalization, Concept Art and Game Design on culturalization, Audio on voice-over, and QA when it comes to platform certification, just to highlight a few key areas of cooperation. As a Producer, you are ideally positioned to facilitate this collaboration between disciplines, ensuring that information is flowing in all directions and the necessary discussions happen.

Early involvement

Localization only happens at the end, once the game is almost completed, so it is something we will only have to think about later, right? Not quite. The foundation for this work is laid down as early as pre-production. Localization should be brought in nice and early so that they can build these foundations. Their timely involvement can prevent serious issues, such as Korean characters appearing as little squares on screen later on, so very close to the release date! Involving localization early also means that their work is incorporated into the project roadmap and there is sufficient time allocated for this. Depending on the scope of the game, this could take weeks or months altogether, and there are upstream dependencies to consider. Just like any other discipline in the game team, localization cannot make things happen in zero time.

"GOOD LOCALIZATION IS EXPENSIVE"

True! But bad localization is even more expensive! Players all over the world have high expectations for game quality, and they expect the same level of immersion as the speakers of the game's source language. Clunky wording can very easily break that immersion and gather some negative reviews from your international players.

And here is the thing: localization is not just one of the cost items in your game budget. At the end of the day, it is the cheapest and safest way to increase revenue once your game is released. There are about 400 million native speakers of English on this planet. Another 1 billion speak it as a second language. And there are approximately 3.3 billion people who play games. Once you've done the maths, you realize that localization is not just a language matter, but a business matter.

To Tamara's point above regarding "early involvement," I have personally handled loc on *Halo Wars 2, Total War: Elysium,* several localized projects at FundamentalVR, and have seen for myself the benefits of early collaboration and preparation when handling localized games. Reaching out early means they can advise your team on setting up pipelines, preparing schedules, and which tools will help you the most. Additionally, I strongly recommend setting up a document at the start of the project to track your text strings as they are implemented. You could do this afterward, of course, but you don't want to go sieving through design scripts, now do you?

BUDGETS

Ok. Here we are. It's time to talk about money. A lot of day-to-day budget management isn't actually discussed in currency, but is converted to work days, staff months, or another abstract unit. These are designed to better match the scheduling language of your business and projects.

Budget planning

As discussed in the milestones section, the initial budget for the game will be a dollar amount agreed at the time of writing a contract. Delivery of this money will likely be spread across multiple milestones and project stages, so the publisher/investors do not pay everything all at once. You will need a documented budget plan, as most publishers/investors won't hand over a penny until they see evidence that someone on your team has an understanding of budgets, and how they will be allocated. This plan should consider:

- Development team wages
- External teams (e.g., outsourcers, localization, external QA, etc.)
- Development hardware and software
- Recruitment
- Marketing
- Support teams costs (e.g., IT, HR, marketing, and brand)
- Office costs (e.g., rent, bills, food, stationery, and furniture)

The better you break down your cost ahead of time, the better equipped you will be to talk about your money. It will help if you can build this larger budget from smaller budgets from each development team. Every team will find new things to spend money on, but here are some examples of unique costs per department:

- **Art** – Model and texture licenses, motion capture studio time/ performers, photogrammetry excursions, render farm hire for cinematics
- **Design** – Purchasing games for competitive analysis, materials for prototypes, fact-finding excursions
- **Audio** – Sound libraries, recording equipment, recording excursions, actors, musicians
- **QA** – External QA. Lots of them
- **Marketing** – Video assets, graphics, interviews, advertising space, travel and demo costs.

Work days? Staff months?

People cost more than just their salaries. When you include all the various taxes, pensions, benefits, training, bonuses, and all the other overheads of keeping a roof over your business, then you realize that people cost a lot of money (sometimes double their actual salary!) If you want to dive into the numbers, I recommend the "True Cost of an Employee Calculator" on good-calculators.com, which will let you play with employee cost breakdowns.

Because these numbers are so complicated it is helpful to have a simplified language for communicating budgets across teams, so the Director of Production and Chief Finance Officer will usually figure out a developer "day rate" based on all the employee and business costs, plus company profits. They will generally translate this budget into "work days" and assign out budgets to teams using this metric. For example, an engineering lead may be given a budget of 2,500 work days for the project, and must now balance the size and cost of his team to fit within that scope, with which the engineering producer will assist. Keep in mind that "Work Days" is initially only designed to budget for internal developers, but if you know your day rate (e.g., 1 work day = $600), then you can translate other costs into work days. Some of these are discussed below.

Contractors, outsourcers, and purchases

When you reach out to contractors and outsourcers they will provide a quote for your work, which you will need to include in your project budget. If they are based in a different economy, then they will likely send that quote in their native currency. Let's say you are working in US dollars and your European contractor sends an invoice for 20,000 euros. You first convert this to 21,663.88 dollars to make it compatible with your business, after which you can divide it by your 600-dollar day rate giving you 36.1 work days.

What about when you need more money?

Don't worry, this happens more often than you think. When you go to your publisher or investors, you will need to answer a few questions to build their confidence, such as:

1. How have you spent what we already gave you?
2. Has any money been wasted?
3. How do we know you're managing the money properly?
4. What will giving you more money achieve?
5. Are we still going to make a profit on this?

How you respond depends on who you are talking to. If you are talking to very money-centric people, then you will want to show your records in detail to reassure them that you pay as much attention to money as they do. If you are talking to more passionate, game-driven people, then you will want to inspire with quality work, and talk of the potential features and player excitement. If you're talking to business developers, then you will want to talk about how this money is essential for market capture, sellable features, and investments for future product cycles.

With game publishers, assume you're dealing with all of the above, and be ready for all sides of questioning. My advice to producers is to build processes that make you ready for these kinds of questions *at any time*. Check in with your budgets regularly, build quotes for future plans, and encourage a stable build pipeline so you can always show someone some cool gameplay if they ask questions.

What does the producer do?

In a small company, the producer might do pretty much all of the above, maybe with the assistance of an external business accountant. However, in most large studios the budget will be compartmentalized per department. For example, the localization producer may have to handle tracking of the loc budget, writing and approving the purchase orders, forecasting the future usage, and advising the production team on budget progress.

If you are like me, and you arrived into the game industry knowing next to nothing about finance, then the numbers involved with game development can be pretty intimidating. However, I have found that the more you break things down into spreadsheets, separate the costs, and handle these numbers in detail, the easier and less scary it gets. Before long, you will be one of those people who knows exactly where all the money is, and people will be coming to *you* for advice. If nothing else, I recommend searching the internet for examples and templates of budgets from game studios and other businesses, and this will help you understand the structure, and give you a place from which to start.

OUTSOURCERS AND CONTRACTORS

This is a catch-all term for anyone working on your game who is not a full-time member of your studio. This can range from a single audio contractor making a handful of sound effects to an entire co-development studio making entire features. Sometimes specialist contractors will be asked to come and work directly inside the studio for a time, meaning they can also share some knowledge and up-skill your team while they are on-site.

Outsourcing work to another company is most appropriate when you have a lot of content that needs to be provided, but only for a small part of the project. As such, the following areas are commonly outsourced:

- 2D art – generic posters and signs
- 3D art – generic environment models
- Audio – specialist sound recording, musicians, and orchestras
- QA – functional testing
- Loc – translation and loc testing

A producer overseeing outsourcing will need to ensure the requirements are clearly agreed with the outsourcer, and then codify this information into a "statement of work." The following questions are important:

- What is their day rate?
- What is their team size?
- Will they be contracted for a number of days, or for specific deliverables?
- What is the high-level delivery and payment schedule?

- What obligations does the hiring studio have to the outsourcer? (e.g., pipelines, equipment, and feedback cadence)
- Who owns the resulting content/code?

Once this document is signed by both parties, the work can begin. The outsourcing producer should monitor and track the completion, acting as the point of contact with the organization. Once the work is delivered, the outsourcer will send an invoice to the company for payment.

While a company is not beholden to the fortunes of its contractors and outsourcers after the contract, it is worth building good working relationships between your team and theirs. If your game is successful, you will likely have the same project needs again, and you may want to hire that same outsourcer. I also advise running retrospectives with your outsourcers after every major deliverable; I have seen many co-development arrangements fail because the hiring company did not have the good practices required to enable smooth outsourcing, so it pays to ensure that your team is ready to handle such an arrangement. Ensure responsibilities are clear, deliverables are clear, and that everyone is supported throughout development, and your studio can enjoy the empowerment that outsourcing can provide.

VERSION CONTROL

If all your files are on just one computer, then one stroke of bad luck could cause you to lose your entire game. This is where version control comes in. Version control – also called source control – is a form of file storage that enables multiple people to work on the same project together. It provides a central location for all the project files and enables a detailed history of each one so that issues can be tracked to a specific change in a specific file. No group software project should begin without setting up source control to keep your project files safe.

Version control gets technical very quickly, but here are some terms that producers should learn:

- **Depot** – Central location where all submitted files are stored
- **Workspace** – The files that are actually on your computer
- **Trunk** – The main development depot where the game should be playable
- **Branches** – A separate depot for when an isolated development environment is needed, risky features or for curating a release build

- **Integrations** – The technically intricate process of moving and merging submissions between trunks and branches
- **Changelists** – The numerical ID assigned to each individual submission. Often communicated between developers and QA to help verify fixes
- **Shelving** – A system for passing your changelist to another developer without submitting to the central depot
- **Buddy Checks** – Having another developer check your code before you submit. The "Pull Request" feature in the Git version control system enforces this practice before you can submit.

A producer won't have to set up the version control on their own, as this will generally be a collaboration between the technical directors, build engineers, and IT. However, a producer should get comfortable working with version control tools, and get familiar with the structure of their team's depot. Many development processes are connected to how the team interacts with their version control, so a producer should be ready to assess this area for process improvements.

REFERENCE

1. Wikipedia contributors. Bug (engineering) [Internet]. Wikipedia, The Free Encyclopedia. 2024. Available from: https://en.wikipedia.org/w/index.php?title=Bug_(engineering)&oldid=1243663585

Breaking in
Getting the job

6

I expect that many people who have picked up this book are looking for their first job in game production. There is naturally a lot of luck involved with finding such a job, and in this chapter, I will share all the ways I can think to improve that luck when diving into the world of work.

CVS AND LINKEDIN

Your curriculum vitae (CV) will be your first key tool to job-hunting in the games industry. The purpose of a CV is to make it as easy as possible for a potential employer to understand your range and depth of skills and experience, with as little reading as possible. Some CVs extend to two pages, but early in your career I would aim to keep it to a single page, and you can cycle out older, less relevant experiences as you proceed.

There are many ways to add things to CVs, and a lot of different CV cultures around the world differ (e.g., photo/no photo, more pages/fewer), but here are some key elements:

- **Your preferred name** – I recently rebranded from "Douglas" to "Doug" online, as it's what everybody calls me anyway.
- **Email** – No employer wants to email grumpytoad2008@troublmak. er. Make an email address with your name.
- **LinkedIn profile link** – Make yourself easy to find.
- **Summary** – Keep it short and show your career intentions. For example, "An aspiring producer, with experience in managing teams, looking to build AAA game industry knowledge and create great video games."
- **Professional experience** – Any jobs or volunteer positions you've had, including:

DOI: 10.1201/9781003519065-6

- Role title and employer
- When you were in this role (e.g., January 2026–October 2027)
- A short list of the responsibilities, and what you learned while performing them.

- **Skills** – e.g., Google suite, Jira, conflict resolution, project-planning, etc. Only put skills that you are ready to answer questions about.
- **Education** – Only university-level education and above. This section becomes less and less relevant over time, but can still be a conversation starter in the interview ("Oh, you went to blah blah University? Did you know Mr. Blahson? He teaches there!")
- **Certifications** – Any external certifications that are relevant to your career (e.g., SCRUM Master I).
- **Accolades** – If you have any interesting awards, titles, competition prizes, or similar. They help give a sense of your active and productive character.
- **Hobbies and interests** – People like hiring humans, so it's worth including a couple of things that help them connect to you this way (e.g., rock-climbing, cooking, and reading.).

LinkedIn has become a very powerful tool in game industry recruiting, so it's essential to have a good profile there. Put your chosen name for your industry, a clear photo of yourself, and an industry-relevant cover photo. Producers tend not to have websites or art portfolios, so your LinkedIn will likely be your professional homepage. Also, a tip for conferences: print off your LinkedIn profile QR code and slide it into your conference pass, so people can connect with you right there as you meet them.

You can also save your LinkedIn profile to PDF, and it will automatically create a tidy, well-formatted CV. I must have read dozens of CVs that were exported from LinkedIn before I realized that they were generated that way, so I can vouch for the fact that hiring managers don't care how they're made, just as long as they are clear, concise, and readable. You can use this to optimize your LinkedIn; create your profile, add your experience, export to PDF to see what the CV looks like, then update the profile to add the right bits of depth until the CV export is to your liking.

NETWORKING STARTS NOW

Game development is a community, and you'll want to find the way in that is right for you. Networking isn't just those "industry mixer" events that you see organized online or at conferences; networking is anything that helps you meet new people, be it a drinks event, a conference, a masterclass, a Discord server, or a game jam. Every single person you meet is a potential future employer, employee, or peer. In 2011, I met a man called Thom Kaczmarek at a game jam, and created some music for him that weekend. Twelve years later in 2023 he invited me to a college student showcase to meet his VR students and talk to them about their games. Similarly, I got a voice-acting role on the game *Death and Taxes* (Placeholder Gameworks, 2020) because I'd met the creative lead on the 2019 Train Jam and given her a business card. Six months later she reached out and invited me to audition. Networking is a long game.

When you meet people in the industry remember to be courteous and curious; ask them about their development, their experience, and show some genuine interest in their career. Be ready to explain your interests, skills, experience, and next career steps, so they have a chance to think of you if a good opportunity comes up. Acting like you already know everything is a sign of arrogance that will put everyone off, so show that you are keen to learn and grow, particularly early in your career. Not everyone may enjoy meeting new people all the time, but each time you have an in-person interaction with someone you become so much more than "just another CV" and they may be able to recommend you for roles, tell you about opportunities, or just be a positive presence in your future. Also, networking never really stops. You have decades of career ahead of you, and the opportunities for new collaborations will forever evolve. Opportunities come from relationships, so start building good ones.

DOES ANYONE READ COVER LETTERS? YES. I DO

I often hear people say that cover letters aren't important, and that no-one reads them anyway. I disagree, because when I'm the hiring manager I absolutely read cover letters. They give the applicant an opportunity to show me their written communication skills, their ability to articulate their experience, and it can show me if they have already built an understanding of the role they are applying for. Many times an applicant's cover letter has got my attention where their CV did not.

When reading your cover letter I'm expecting you to answer three questions in the space of one page:

1. Why do you want this job?
2. What experiences prepared you for the responsibilities in this job?
3. What can I expect if I hire you?

Answering these questions will show me that you have a clear understanding of how you and the role are a good match.

If I don't read the cover letter there could be several reasons; I didn't have enough time, the file got lost in the hiring pipeline, or something else, but don't let the reason I didn't read your cover letter be that *you didn't write one.* Even if no one ever reads these cover letters, the act of writing down your ambitions, qualifying your experiences, and selling yourself will improve your own understanding of you as a professional, and can build both confidence and competence.

DOES A "PRODUCER PORTFOLIO" EVEN EXIST?

Production is not like art, audio, or game design in that you can't just submit a portfolio of your creations. In fact, it's often very hard to quantify what a producer contributes to a project at all; the most competent producers create environments in which there is no drama and there's not actually much to talk about, whereas incompetent producers can be seen struggling and prevailing over an everlasting fire that they never seem to put out.

This leads me to what makes up a portfolio for producers: the problems you permanently solved. As you go through your career, start taking notes on each problem you manage to completely take away, and reflect on how you approached that problem, analyzed it, and remedied it. Some examples may look like this:

- Audio teams had constantly changing workloads because features were always changing at the design level, and no one was communicating. You reached out to the design team and found that they had no idea this was causing a problem. You decided to arrange a regular sync meeting to discuss upcoming features and impacts between the two teams, and the problem has gone away.
- People were always submitting requests to the tech support team without crucial information, meaning that every single request needed several follow-up conversations before anyone could even start fixing the problem. You decided that a form in Slack could solve this, as it could ask for the important information up front, eliminating most of the follow-up conversations. You collaborated with the tech support team, built the form, and coached the developers in using it. Support response delays have dropped noticeably since.

Solving problems includes everything from arranging an effective meeting to improve communication, to creating a new tool to reduce human error, to starting a regular report to create better project transparency, and more. Think of the little things you're proud of in your work and that can help you find these portfolio pieces, which can then become part of your CV, your cover letters, and your conversations with prospective employers.

WHERE DO I LOOK FOR JOBS?

Finding jobs has changed so many times since I started my career that it's dizzying, so here's a spread of everything I've seen tried in my career to find opportunities:

- **Game studio websites and social media** – First thing to do is check out your favorite game studios and see whether they have any jobs on their website. You should also follow them on any social media they have, as it'll be the quickest way to see if anything new comes up.
- **LinkedIn searches and alerts** – You can search on LinkedIn for certain types of jobs, specifying the location, company, experience level, and so on. You can then set these to regular alerts, so you will get immediately notified if a new job matching your interests gets posted.
- **Game job boards and mailing lists** – I recommend a web search to find as many of these as you can, but some that I've used in the past are:
  - jobs.gamesindustry.biz
  - gamesjobsdirect.com
  - ingamejob.com
  - WorkWithIndies.com (indie devs only)
  - remotegamejobs.com (remote roles only)
  - otta.com (games and tech)
- **Recruiters** – Recruitment agencies often already have a relationship built with your chosen company and can be a human advocate for your initial application. Look for a game recruitment agency website, set up a profile with your CV, and they will contact you if they think they have a role that matches you (recruiters will often

call on the phone, these things can happen fast!) Make sure your LinkedIn is set to "Open To Work" as recruiters get alerts about these profiles and might reach out to you first.

- **Online communities** – There's at least one "Game Production" Discord server out there, and production jobs often get shared in these communities. These are also good learning and networking environments.
- **Your contacts** – This is where the networking pays off. If you have friends in game studios, make sure they know you're looking for production roles. If there is a role at their studio, they can likely get a referral bonus if they recommend you.
- **Speculative emails** – Find the recruitment officer at your favorite studios and send them your CV and cover letter anyway. I've seen it work.

Which is the best one to use? Whichever one gets you the job. Use them all. And even if you're not sure you're qualified, apply anyway, and let the employer be the one that says no, rather than yourself. Don't limit your own opportunities.

THE INTERVIEW

Okay! You've got their attention! It's interview time!

Your CV has shown that you might have the functional qualifications to do the job, but the interview is more about relationships – this is about them figuring out if they can work with you as a person. Each place you interview for will be figuring out what the essential qualities are for their role, as studios, teams and projects will differ. Before I provide any advice, it will make sense to examine what the hiring manager is looking for during the interview.

Promising signs

Here are some "green flags" I consider when I'm interviewing production candidates. Some of these only apply to online interviews, but the principles carry over:

- On time and prepared, with working audio and video.
- Polite and respectful to me and my colleagues.
- Can go into depth about areas of experience, giving examples and discussing lessons.

- Honest about where they lack experience.
- Have read the role description, studied my company, and clearly understand what I want from the role.
- Know what they want from the role personally.
- Have plenty of questions.
- Show an interest in learning.
- Can carry a conversation.

Preparation

With all the above considered, you should take the following steps when preparing for interviews:

- Read the role description in depth, and compare it to your own CV and experience.
- Study the company's recent work to understand the context for the role.
- If possible, spend some time playing some of their games to understand their products first-hand.
- Figure out what you want from that company and role, how you want to develop, and what you want to learn.
- Come up with some questions for the interviewers. Good topics are production tools, processes, team structures, company lifestyle, and anything else that will help you make your decision.
- Have an idea of the salary you're after. You can find average salaries for the role and location online (e.g., statista.com). Don't be afraid that they will stop returning your calls if your first ask is too high, as salaries *always* go through a negotiation process. Always ask above your minimum.

Producer tests

More and more I am seeing companies do some kind of "producer test," which will generally be designed to check for a very specific skill-set, or check the applicants competence in a very common scenario. Here are some examples of producer tests I have encountered:

- **Data handling exercise** – Applicant was given a curated set of project data, asked to visualize it, call out any problems they could see, and suggest courses of action.

- **Written essay on mentoring** – Applicant was asked to write a couple of pages on a time when they mentored a colleague, discussing their reasons for mentoring them, the methods they used, and the outcomes.
- **Role-playing a scenario** – Applicant was given the task to plan a three-week sprint for three engineers, and told to figure out the rest. They then had to ask the interviewers questions in their "roles" (e.g., art lead and engineering lead) to get requirements, negotiate the conflicting priorities, and come up with a viable plan. This assessed their ability to proactively gather the information needed for a viable plan.

These tests will be the clearest indicator you can get for what the job will be like, and can be a good decider for yourself if it seems like the job you want. As you are going through all these interviews remember that you aren't begging for a role; you are looking for a business partnership for the next step in your career, and you should be prepared to say "No" if the role is not looking to be the right move for you, whether that's because of the salary, the requirements, or even the character of the people who interview you. Take your time, and find the right role for you.

Interviewing your own producers

One day you may interview producers yourself, for which I also have a few key tips:

- **Study the applicant** – Read through their CV, cover letter, and LinkedIn, and discuss their apparent strengths and experience with other producers.
- **Figure out what you want to know** – What will help you make your decisions? Maybe it's their production methodologies, or their personal character, or their technical skills. Decide in advance.
- **Plan your approach** – How will you start the interview? Who will ask which questions? How will you finish? When will you ask for *their* questions? Have a plan that will help you conduct the interview your way.
- **Be prepared** – Make sure you're ready to welcome the applicant, with working sound and video, and have their CV and cover letter on hand.
- **Let the conversation flow** – Production is a communication-based role, so it is valuable to let the conversation flow naturally where

possible, with occasional steering if you want to ask about something specific. This will give you the most accurate representation of what working with them will be like; producer jobs are not about answering test questions, they're about talking.

- **Be courteous and respectful** – You are representing your company, and it pays to show respect to every applicant, even if you choose not to employ them.
- **Send rejection feedback** – If an employee gets as far as an interview, I consider it respectful to send personalized feedback. In doing so are both investing in the future of game producers, as well as sending them away with a good experience of your company. Yes, you're rejecting them, but it's much more humane than sending a copied and pasted "no."

WHAT SALARY SHOULD I ASK FOR?

It's normal to feel awkward the first few times you're asked "What are your salary expectations?"

It's extremely rare that a company has a rigid, public structure for what their wages are, as the job market is built on an endless cycle of negotiation, offers, and counter-offers. With that in mind, there are a few steps you can take to give yourself some more conviction when pitching your expected salary:

Do the research

Although there is still something of a taboo around discussing your personal salary, there are some resources online which give a sense of the general state of game industry wages:

- **InGame Job** – Has a salary calculator based on their annual "Big Salary Survey," which you can filter down to your department and experience level
- **GameIndustryCareerGuide** – Has a "Video Game Developer Salary" report that is updated every six months
- **Glassdoor** – Contains a lot of self-reported information about salaries across all industries. You can search for your desired location and position (I suggest the term "Game Producer" for accuracy), and you will see the range of reported salaries in that area.

Consider your needs

Forgetting experience and creation of value for a moment, you will need a salary that can handle your cost of living, so it will make sense to figure this out. Rent, bills, food, travel, and dependents should all be considered when calculating your wage needs. Cost of living also varies greatly by region, and cities are generally more expensive to live in than rural areas. A common guideline is to spend no more than 30% of your income on rent, which may sound difficult in the world's more expensive cities, but spending more than this will put a strain on your other costs of living.[1] You can look at rent heat maps online to help you find the more affordable areas, and factor this into your salary requirements.

Ask high, and let them negotiate you down

I think I have a problem with self-valuation, as I have *never* had a prospective employer negotiate my salary down, meaning that I could probably have asked for more every time! Negotiation is very normal in deciding salaries, and employers are used to it. Don't be afraid that an employer will turn you down because of your first offer; if they are interested in you they will always go for a counter-offer first. You're not begging for a job, you're entering into a mutually beneficial working partnership.

"THE QA ROUTE"

There are lots of different career pathways that lead to becoming a game producer, but one of the most common so far has been via "the QA route." These are people that have spent several years in game QA before applying internally or externally for a game producer role. I spent the first five years of my career in game QA and audio QA before getting an interest in the production department and applying for my first production role. This is a historically successful path, as much of the QA pipeline provides excellent foundational experience for a new producer, and shows them the testing, reporting, fixing, and releasing pipelines that they will later be tasked with facilitating. It also gives a detailed insight into the entire game product, along with many of the same tools they will be using in a production role. A seasoned QA tester will be well-versed in the rhythm of a project, common risk areas, and the communication pipelines for managing a large team. All of these are excellent experience pieces for producers.

I expect some change to this, as there are more and more quality courses around the world specifically for game producers, meaning more university graduates that are immediately ready for game production jobs. However, I do expect that many seasoned game QA professionals may notice their aspirations shifting toward the production side of game development, and this path will remain competitive and viable. The only caveat I will give here is that an aspiring producer should not apply for a QA role unless they are ready to 100% commit to QA responsibilities in that time. No QA manager wants to hire someone who is just looking to escape to another field, but they are looking for people who are willing to spend time learning, performing, and delivering on the QA team.

COMING FROM ANOTHER INDUSTRY

To close this chapter I'll briefly address the challenge of transitioning to the game industry as an experienced professional in a nongaming field. Many producers come in from other industries, such as software, advertising, and industrial engineering. It is a completely viable transition, but there is advice to give, all the same.

My first piece of advice is to take stock of your skills. My assumption is that most of these people's experience will be rooted in project management, and that they will have been learning techniques, skills, and methodologies that relate most closely to their industry. From here, my first piece of advice is to reflect on your methodologies and practices, ensuring you know *why* they are applied and how to recognize the problems they solve. You will likely encounter familiar problems in the game industry to your own – resource management, difficult stakeholders, communication challenges, and so on. If you can identify these same problems, you can apply the same tools. However, if the problems facing you are different, then some of the methodologies may need to stay on the shelf. The most obvious examples are agile software development practices; these can completely transform game studios with smaller, faster-iteration products that are agile-compatible, but when applied to R&D projects, huge interdependent waterfall games, or indie passion projects, these practices can create lots of overhead with no actual product improvement. A phrase to remember when bringing your practices over is "apply when applicable."

My second piece of advice is to learn about game developers. A game studio may look like a huge software company, but they are creatives first, and will all have been founded on the premise of producing innovative games at good quality. There may be high-level execs who are holding you accountable for seeking profit and spend, but the majority of game developers will only be interested in your help if the ultimate goal is quality, so you should work this motivation into the justification of all your processes. "This will save us thousands of dollars" will carry far less weight than "This will help us make the game even better."

My last piece of advice is to learn about players. They will be unlike any customers you have ever dealt with, responding with the utmost joy when the release is good, and burning with the most damning criticism when things go wrong. In the game industry, testing a product iteration means playing the game, tapping into your own understanding of how you have fun, and communicating this to other people. In order to understand the player, you will have to become one as part of your job. The players are why we do it, and they will be relying on you to help get it done.

REFERENCE

1. McMullen L, Sheehy K. How much of your income should go to rent? I [Internet]. NerdWallet. 2020 [cited 2024 Oct 2]. Available from: https://www.nerdwallet.com/article/finance/how-much-should-i-spend-on-rent

What's my task? *producer responsibilities*

7

As you may be tired of reading, every producer role is going to be different and will vary in day-to-day activities, practices, and working environments. However, the expectations of producers do have a degree of consistency across the industry, and many of them are hired to meet the same basic need, which is to keep things running. This chapter will break down some of the responsibilities you can expect to be held accountable to at different stages of your projects.

YOUR FIRST WEEK IN THE JOB

Your first week in a new production role is all about getting settled into a company. You will likely be welcomed either by your manager or by a member of the human resources (HR) team who will show you around the office. You'll get an HR induction to go over all the company processes such as holidays, sick pay, benefits, and points of contact, and then an information technology (IT) induction where they explain the building IT and security systems to you, as well as giving you your building access card.

Once the company introductions are done, next comes role onboarding. Your manager will likely arrange some introductory meetings with the team, talk you through the projects, tools, and departments, and discuss your first responsibilities. They may immediately introduce you to the team you'll be supporting, or they may advise that you spend a week or so shadowing another producer; you would join their meetings, ask them questions, and look over the work they do to get a sense of how the job flows. During this time you should fully engage your curiosity, and learn everything you can about the environment. Ask for documentation to read, request to join as

DOI: 10.1201/9781003519065-7

many meetings as you can, and set up introduction meetings with adjacent staff members (30 minutes is usually enough per person) so you can get to know the people as quickly as possible.

In most companies you won't be expected to have much impact in the first couple of weeks, but after that you will likely be given a sub-team to assist with task estimation and scheduling, or a process to start tracking. My first production responsibilities on *Halo Wars 2* were scheduling the VFX and audio teams and facilitating the localization pipeline, and it took many months of questions and stumbling before I was on top of these. Getting started is daunting, but remember to be patient with yourself, keep learning, and ask for help when you need it.

CONCEPTING PHASE RESPONSIBILITIES

During the concepting phase, the goal of the production is to help the team get ready for preproduction. The development team will be looking to explore the ideas for their game, and a producer can look to help out in the following ways:

- Facilitating brainstorming sessions among the departments, ensuring they have the materials they need to conduct the sessions, and that all the information is logged and shared afterward.
- Drafting project schedules and resource plans, starting from the top-level contract schedule and steadily adding more detail as more information is known.
- Discussing the methodologies and tools that will be used to manage the project.
- Brainstorming the project and team responsibilities, and ensuring that they are all agreed upon by the leadership groups. (This will be covered more in the section on the "RASCI" document.)
- Preparing the preproduction plan, which should include:
  - The prototypes that need building
  - The art and audio reference material that needs gathering
  - The tools, software, and equipment that need acquiring
  - The team members who need hiring

By the end of this phase, the team should be able to start hiring all of their desired team members, and start digging into the brainstormed ideas in detail.

PREPRODUCTION PHASE RESPONSIBILITIES

Following the concepting phase, there should be a high level idea of the game, but with a lot of questions remaining, and in preproduction all those questions need answering. Producers should ensure that these outstanding questions are clearly communicated among the team leads and directors, so the goals of preproduction are agreed upon. By the end of preproduction, there should be a solid plan for production in which the team can be confident of success.

During preproduction a producer will often have a department or game area to support. This can be:

- Arranging collaborative sessions between departments to generate and explore ideas
- Get dependencies discussed
- Build cost, resource, and timeline projections
- Ensure that all decisions are broadcast to the team
- Working development decisions into the project backlog
- Coordinate playtesting of prototypes

The production team should also be ensuring that their own communication pipelines, methods, and tools are ready to handle the production phase and that the team will be able to follow the plan. Examples of production areas to prepare include:

- Project documentation structure
- Communication channels (e.g., Slack, Teams, Discord, etc.)
- User groups for software (chat, emails, security access, etc.)
- Task and bug tracking software
- Reporting needs and routines
- Detailed schedule of milestone deliverables
- Development routines (e.g., sprints, reviews, and planning events)
- Daily, weekly, and monthly meeting schedules
- Interviewing and hiring new producers to complete the production team
- Defining the responsibilities of the production team

One of the hardest parts of preproduction is ending it at the right time. Every game industry veteran will have a story of a project that accelerated into production before they were ready, sprinting off in the wrong direction and getting even further from the finish line than they started. In game development, this results in lost time, cut features, and a team that burns out trying to save half a game before the money runs out. The clearer you can make the preproduction criteria, the easier it will be to ensure you only go into production when you're ready.

PRODUCTION PHASE RESPONSIBILITIES

Once you're in production, and the major planning work is complete, the focus will shift executing those plans as efficiently as possible. The teams shift from "think tank" mode into "content factory" mode, and so the production teams shift their support toward ensuring velocity is maintained, problems are resolved quickly, and steering decisions are made effectively with good information.

Here are some groupings of the main production responsibilities during the production phase:

Tracking and forecasting

Using your chosen task-tracking pipelines, you will be monitoring how fast the backlog of work is being completed. You may do this on a scale of a two-week sprint, on a three-month milestone charge, or on the scale of the entire production phase. Any time you see work is being completed slower than expected, you should be stepping in to identify the cause of the slowdown. If there is a problem, then try and get it resolved, but if this appears to be the realistic pace of the work, then you will need to adjust your expectations for completion, and communicate this to the production team. It could be that features need cutting, the team needs increasing, or a deadline needs shifting.

Scheduling

Just because preproduction is over, it doesn't mean the scheduling is done. As the production phase proceeds, you will be monitoring the pace of your team, the dependencies, and the evolving priorities and updating your schedules to reflect. Make sure the late-stage activities are getting booked in advance, such as user-testing, localization, and QA testing.

Another very important part of scheduling is *telling everyone what the schedule is*. When dates change for a feature, send a wide update informing the team of the changes. Expect to repeat yourself many times; game developers are often very focused on their work and are trusting the production team to watch the clock for them, so when there's a deadline approaching, make sure to remind people several times ahead of the date.

Preventing "feature creep"

"Feature creep" is when a suggestion becomes a workload without going through a planning process. Game teams are full of creative minds and the ideas will never stop coming. While this is essential for innovation, these ideas need to be discussed with the wider team and assessed for viability, both from a schedule perspective and for technical compatibility. Sometimes feature creep also comes from the *way* someone approaches a task. An example could be a programmer deciding that picking up a weapon requires a full multislot inventory system to handle, which creates surprise work for coders, designers, and artists.

DAVID BOWMAN – CHIEF OPERATING OFFICER AT XR GAMES

My first producer would often say "I want a pony." It was a response to me asking for something unachievable. The idea was that if you were in his family, and you said to him "I want a pony" his job would then be to get you to understand everything it takes to get a pony into an 18th floor apartment and look after it; the money, the time and the logistics. It isn't a "No," it's information that helps you decide what to do. Look out for the danger phrases "Wouldn't it be cool if?" and "This should work." These are the occasions where I learned to hold up the mirror to people's requests, and help them make their decisions, just by reflecting on what it will take to achieve them.

Reporting

On larger teams there will be several layers of decision-making. Developers decide their own code lines and brush strokes, leads decide the feature directions and solutions, and directors decide on the main development priorities and project strategy. To enable good-decision making at all levels, the production team should ensure that there is regular and *effective* reporting taking place. This reporting will likely cover team velocities, feature completion, budget spend, as well as any risks and problems being managed.

Onboarding

All those recruits interviewed during the preproduction phase will be duly arriving during the production phase and will need proper onboarding. Before they arrive you should be checking that their equipment has been ordered, their accounts and permissions have been created, and that their lead is ready to receive them. You should set up an onboarding message, email, or online document containing all the links they need, introduce them to all main collaborators, and invite them to a few initial meetings to get them immersed in the team and project. Once they have been around for a while (maybe a month), consider sending them a short survey asking about their onboarding experience, what went well, and what could be improved for the next recruit, which will help improve the process.

Communication assistance

The production team should be experts in communication, and the wider team may need to lean on this expertise at times. Lots of information need to effectively (and continuously) travel across the team, and the production team should be ensuring these information channels are maintained and kept effective. Make sure mailgroups are kept up-to-date, create new message channels when needed, answer questions quickly, and whatever else is needed to keep information flowing. You may also need to assist the team with complex conversations, such as negotiating priorities and defusing conflicts. Everyone needs to communicate, but it's specifically your job to be *good* at it.

Problem-solving

With every exciting new game comes exciting new problems. There is no end to the kind of problems that could come between your team and their progress; hardware failures, software outages, miscommunications, pipeline bottlenecks, unavailable staff members, uncooperative coffee machines, and so on. Whatever the problem is, the production team has a responsibility to ensure that it is solved. This doesn't mean that producers have to know how to solve everything, but they have to arrange the solution; you won't fix the computer, but you'll chase up the IT team for help; you can't stand in for the missing staff members, but you can rearrange lower priority work to free up other people. Whatever the problem your team has, you should be prepared to own it until the solution is found so the team can keep moving.

Protecting the team

A big part of being a producer is about protecting the team from the complications that can beset a project. If there are sudden changes in direction, periods of downtime, or if the team sleepwalks into running out of time on a feature the developers will suffer the consequences of overtime, burnout, and failing morale. The production team should shield the team from these problems, balancing workload to reduce team pressure, keeping information transparent, and ensuring that people know the production team has their back.

Morale

Game projects can be long, and it can be easy to forget the progress being made while fighting all the fires. The production team should look for opportunities to raise morale on a regular basis such as feature completion videos, playtest tournaments, and milestone-release parties (remember to include the remote staff). Make a fuss when new staff members join, so people can get excited about the growing team and community, and if a staff member is leaving, then make a big deal of celebrating their time on the team, as people are generally lifted up when they see their friends celebrated and respected. Remember that morale works differently across different cultures, so what may lift everyone up in an American studio may roll eyes in a European studio, and vice versa.

ALPHA PHASE RESPONSIBILITIES

Alright, you've crossed the ocean, now it's time to land this plane.

Bringing an end to a game project can be a daunting and tense part of the project; you may have dozens of teams of game developers around you working away on their dream project, and now you somehow have to tell them to stop. When approaching the finish line, here's what your responsibilities will likely include:

Ending development gracefully

To help the developers find a natural end, you should keep the Alpha/Feature Complete deadline as clear as possible; this being the point at which all the game's features should be functioning and playable, albeit with some bugs. If the developers know the time remaining clearly, then they will be empowered to make decisions. As you approach the Alpha date, you should also be reporting on the "Feature Complete" status, so the directors can know if they need to step in and help get any difficult decisions made.

Ideally, you will have every feature hit the Alpha date and be "Feature Complete," but if any miss the date they should be managed as exceptions to the rule until they are done. In the PRINCE2 methodology, there is a principle called "Manage by Exception" which is intended to accommodate the fact that some things don't go perfectly, but can still be managed in a controlled manner.[1]

Gather the list for the game credits

Yep. That's your job too. Ask your UI engineer how they set up the credits screen, so they can advise you how to implement the list and the format required. Then, you can start asking around all your team leads for the required names. You will also need to contact any external companies, contractors, and outsourcers that worked on the game. Make sure to run the credits past the leadership team before implementing it, as they have the final say on the order in which names appear.

Managing polish

Developers will want all the polish time they can get; tweaking the animation speed over here, more level dressing over there, *one last* particle effect in multiplayer, and so on. However, changes come with impacts; those animation tweaks could affect audio, the level dressing could affect NPC pathfinding, and that particle effect could collapse the frame rate in the climactic mission. The best way to handle polish is to play the game as a team and highlight the polish as a group, ensuring each team has the means to support the planned changes. The producer should ensure this is all documented and prioritized, because they will also need to say where the polish stops and the bug-fixing begins.

Facilitate the alpha test plan

During alpha, the QA team will be aiming to validate the status of your features, ensuring that everything is working as the design team and directors intended. Producers can help this process by ensuring that the QA team is adequately furnished with the full list of features, with links to documentation that explain the intended feature behaviors. QA will also be relying on the production team to keep them informed as to when a given feature is development complete and ready for complete testing.

BETA PHASE RESPONSIBILITIES

With the end of alpha comes the end of any feature polish. Now there is nothing to do but find bugs and fix them. There should be no further submissions that are not requested through a bug report.

Bug triage

There will always be more bugs than you can fix, so you will need regular "bug triages" to prioritize the issues and ensure your bug-fixing time is spent as wisely as possible. When a bug is entered into the database, a producer reads the report, weighs up the severity, impacts, and repro rate, then gives the bug a priority (e.g., high, medium, and low). As the release nears, the production team will start marking low-priority bugs as "Won't Fix" to ensure the dwindling time is focused on the biggest issues, and calling an end to the minor fixes.

Supporting QA

The producers will need to ensure the QA team has everything they need to fully cover the game, report their bugs, and communicate effectively with the developers. If the QA team is having a problem, it will generally be reported to production by a QA lead, who will need to source its solution. Many of these problems can relate to how the development team interacts with the bug pipeline, so you should be prepared to educate (and *reeducate*) the development team on the fly to ensure they know how to read bug reports, request additional info, and discuss the fixes.

Supporting localization

The localization team should receive the entire game's worth of text and voice during alpha so that they can power through the translations and return them during beta, ready for loc QA testing. Once all polish is finalized the last text and voice changes should be sent to the localization team so they can update the translated content. During this time loc producer will need to respond to requests for clarifications on terms, assistance with fixing loc bugs, and builds for loc testing. Loc QA testing always finishes last to ensure that all text fixes in the main language are also fixed in the localized product.

RELEASE PHASE RESPONSIBILITIES

Ok, let's do this…

Ship it!

This is it. The polish is done, the bugs are fixed, and the directors, QA, and localization teams have all signed off on the final build, so it's time to release. The production team now needs to hand the build to their designated release manager, who will convey it to the intended platforms. You should ensure that you have key tech staff on standby in case there are any surprises in the submission process that require a speedy fix. If the submission is successful, you can now share the good news with the team. You've shipped the game!

Organize the launch party

Well…someone's got to do it!

Arranging something fun for the team to enjoy together can cement the shared feeling of accomplishment and help cast off the tensions that can build up during the finaling process. When choosing what to do, take some time to think about your team members, and ensure everyone is included and welcome. Remember, not everyone drinks alcohol, not everyone in game development is a gamer, and not everyone can participate in extreme physical activities, so make sure you do the right thing for your team. Oh, and don't just invite the development team; everyone involved from your company should be included (e.g., operations, IT, and legal).

POSTMORTEMS

Well, that was a fun wrap party, but the work continues. There's DLC work already happening, and you've got another major project starting soon. One more responsibility of the production team is to arrange the project retrospective, commonly known as a "postmortem." The goal of a postmortem is to gather as much feedback as possible from the development teams and turn it into actionable lessons that the team can apply.

Postmortems will commonly run along these lines, either in person, or virtually:

Part 1 – Gathering notes

- The team is brought into a room and is briefed on the process by the assigned moderator.
- Each team member writes out a number of sticky notes with things that went well and things that need improvement.
- All notes are added to a shared board.
- Team members vote on the notes they deem most important.
- The votes define the priority of each note.

Part 2 – Suggestions and actions

- The team discusses each note in priority order (you rarely get through them all) and suggest solutions.
- The moderator then writes these into actions and gives them owners.
- After the session the moderator documents the results and shares them with the leadership teams.

Part 3 – Analysis

- The leadership team will analyze the postmortem results and consider actions from their own perspective.
- These actions should then be communicated to the wider team with clear owners and timelines wherever possible.
- Ideally, the production team will regularly follow up on these actions to ensure all lessons are being incorporated into working practice.

Running postmortems is challenging. They can be very emotional times, with a lot of bottled-up frustrations being vented, and the team will be expecting you to get everything fixed. To help you prepare for these, here are the tips I have picked up from running these sessions:

- **Prepare well** – Plan the postmortem process in advance, and practice it throughout development regular retrospectives.
- **Include some "no leaders" sessions** – Sometimes the honest feedback will only come if the room is a safe and unintimidating space, without the leadership team present.
- **Consider getting an external moderator** – At Creative Assembly we would often use an external, impartial consultant to facilitate our project postmortems, which helped the team rationally process their frustrations into actionable feedback and objective lessons.
- **Plan the follow-up mechanism** – You can gather all the feedback you like, but it's wasted if you never act on it, so my advice is to work the actions into your weekly production team meetings so they are regularly reviewed and dealt with.
- **Stay calm** – These sessions can get emotional, and as a facilitator you will need to stay calm and controlled, which creates the space for other people to open up.

SCHEDULES AND SCENARIOS

One of the main responsibilities of producers up and down the team involves creating schedules. This could be a high-level milestone schedule, covering the whole project, a feature development schedule covering a few months, or a two-week schedule covering the day-to-day work of an agile team. Let's look at the basics:

Why do we make schedules?

A schedule is made because the project is constrained somehow. Perhaps you are making a game to coincide with another event (e.g., a movie release), in which case the project is constrained by time, and a schedule is needed to ensure a project that can be completed by the given date. Or, perhaps you have no deadline, but the project budget is limited, so you have to be able to create a schedule that meets all the goals without exceeding the staff budget.

Of course, some games are made with no schedule at all. These are generally indie passion projects in which there is no deadline, and no cost, because the developers are doing it all in their spare time. This can also happen in environments where there is so much money that the budget will effectively never run out. Valve Software famously takes as long as they please making projects, because their income from the Steam platform is comfortably sustainable. Incidentally, it is rare to see job adverts for producers at small indie studios or at Valve.

What does a schedule need?

An effective schedule has several components:

- **Deliverables** – The features and content required at a given time
- **Start dates** – When each deliverable is to be started
- **Delivery dates** – When each deliverable is expected to be delivered
- **Relevant events** – Any events that could impact, or rely upon the deliverables, such as conferences, expos, and stakeholder reviews
- **Owners** – This could be the team owning the feature, the producer point of contact, or the individual developer doing the work
- **Dependencies** – For example, the schedule should recognize that dialogue is dependent on script, which is dependent on design
- **Assumptions** – For example, you may be assuming that you will have all new hires by September, that there will only be six multiplayer levels, or that the initial designs are approved within two weeks.

Common schedule formats

Here are three common ways of presenting a schedule, which can be appropriate at different times:

Table schedule (Figure 7.1)

Date	Milestone	Deliverables
30-May-2025	MS1	Level 1 - Design, Concept Art Character 1 - Concept Art Character 2 - Concept Art Menus - UI Blockout Combat - Design
29-Aug-2025	MS2	Level 1 - Environment Art Level 2 - Design, Concept Art Character 1 - 3D Model Character 2 - 3D Model Character 3 - Concept Art Character 4 - Concept Art Menus - Code, UI Art Combat - Code, UI Blockout
27-Nov-2025	MS3	Level 1 - VFX, Audio Level 2 - Environment Art Level 3 - Design, Concept Art Character 1 - Animation Character 2 - Animation Character 3 - 3D Model Character 4 - 3D Model Menus - Audio Combat - UI Art, VFX Art
27-Feb-2026	MS4	Level 1 - QA Level 2 - VFX, Audio Level 3 - Environment Art Character 1 - Audio Character 2 - Audio Character 3 - Animation Character 4 - Animation Menus - QA Combat - Audio

FIGURE 7.1 An example table schedule.

- Simple to create
- No special tools required
- Can store a lot of information
- Usually have the date on the left, then the deliverable summary to the right

Visual timeline (Figure 7.2)

- More pleasing to the eye than the table
- More intuitive way to communicate the passage of time
- Allow for easy illustration of nuance, and additional events if necessary
- Can still include a lot of information, but less text than the table
- Looks great in a slide deck (this example was made in Google Slides)

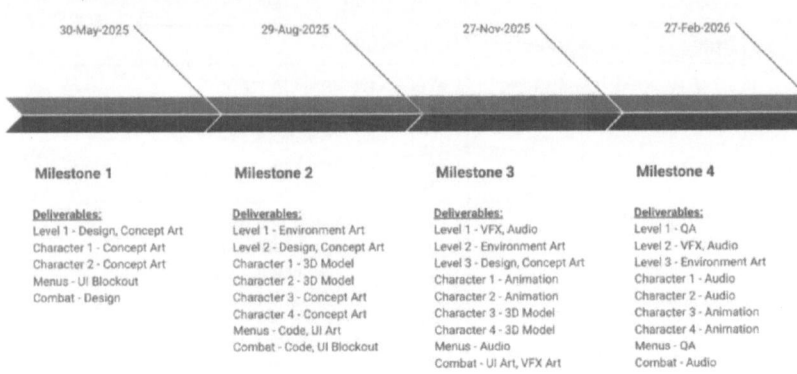

FIGURE 7.2   An example visual timeline.

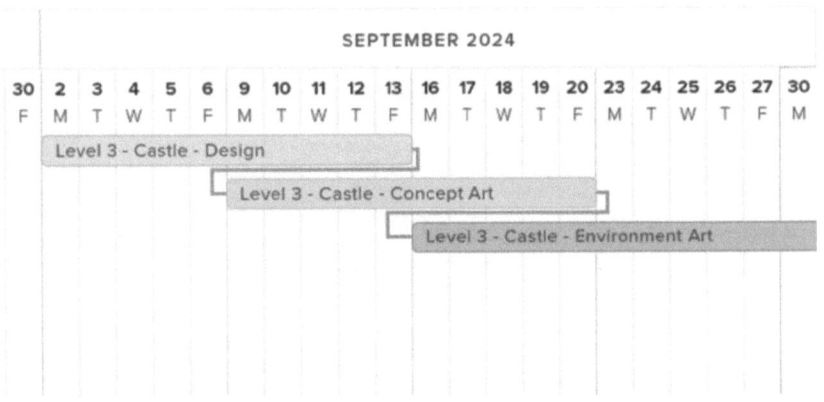

FIGURE 7.3   An example Gantt chart.

Gantt chart (Figure 7.3)

- Designed to show detailed waterfall schedules
- Task length is shown visually
- Lines between tasks indicate dependencies
- Incorporated into many project management tools and directly reads from project data (I made this example using the TeamGantt powerup in Trello)
- Very popular among game development teams

Schedules with different scenarios

Many times you will need to provide a schedule in challenging circumstances; perhaps it has been identified that there is not enough time or resource to complete all the desired work, and the stakeholders need to decide what to do. Creating multiple schedules with different scenarios is an effective way to help the stakeholders make decisions quickly. Here is an example of some different scenarios for the same feature delivery schedule:

- **Scenario A – Reduce feature scope**
  - Actions: We cut the lower priority features we expect to miss the deadline, and deliver the remaining features at the current rate.
  - Impacts: Content is cut from the game.
- **Scenario B – Extend deadline**
  - Actions: We deliver all the features at the current rate, but extend the deadline by one month to accommodate all features.
  - Impacts: Budget increases by $X, next project delayed by one month.
- **Scenario C – Add resource**
  - Actions: We add two more gameplay programmers to accelerate the team, keeping the same feature scope and deadlines.
  - Impacts: Budget increases by $Y, some additional overhead for the feature lead.

Presenting scenarios that clearly state the actions and impacts allows the stakeholders to make a confident decision based on their priorities, which you can then action.

ESTIMATING WORK

In order to create a schedule, you will need an idea of how long all the work will take. That involves estimating the work with your team, which isn't always as straightforward as it sounds.

Here are some points to consider when gathering estimates for your backlog:

Why do we have to estimate everything?

Trust me, someone will ask you this. Estimating tasks can be an annoying distraction from the work people would rather be doing, so it will help if you can lead with the reason and – crucially – how it helps them directly. Here are the reasons I have got used giving:

- It creates better features by helping production to protect the resources required to deliver a feature properly.
- It creates a better game by helping production to manage the scope so that fewer features will be done, but to completion, rather than lots of half-made content.
- It enables a better working life by helping production to protect developers from overtime.
- It enables the studio to make a profit by allowing the team to plan within a limited budget.

Some people need to think out loud

Some experienced developers are very comfortable with estimating tasks, and when you ask "how long will this take?" will frown in thought for a few seconds before answering "2 days." However, a lot of the time developers will need a bit more patience before you get your simple answer. I find a lot of people need to monologue for a while to make enough sense of the idea before they can give a time estimate. This may try your patience, but if someone doesn't know, then they don't know. Let them calculate.

Give rough guidance

Estimates don't need to be exact, otherwise they'd be called "measurements." Developers can get frustrated being asked to nail down something uncertain and will insist "I don't know" when you ask how long a task will take. You can often help with this by giving some approximate sizes; ask them if it's going to be closer to 1 hour, one day, or one week, and they will usually be able to pick one of these. An estimate to this level of detail is generally good enough when you're building a backlog of hundreds of tasks. Some people use a "t-shirt sizes" method, of simply asking whether a task is small, medium, or large.

"Yesterday's weather"

"Yesterday's weather" is a phrase from Agile software development, which comes from the principle that the best way to predict your upcoming work is to look at your most recent work. In SCRUM, the amount of work completed in a sprint will inform the amount of work expected to be completed in the following sprint. This principle can also be adopted for task estimates wherever you have project data; if you have data showing that the average time your team took to model a car was eight days, then it's fairly realistic to expect that future cars will take a similar amount of time.

Contingency

Assume everything will take longer than you expect. If someone says "2 or 3 days," take the bigger number. If someone seems uncertain about their estimate, double it. Then, when the backlog is fully estimated, set up your tracking graphs so they multiply the whole thing by 1.5 (actually we used 1.6 at Creative Assembly), and scope your game to the constrained number. This will always help your team; either the extra time will be used up by problems, or everything goes absolutely fine, and you get more time for polish and bug-fixing.

Days or story points?

In my experience most PC and console game studios do their estimates in days, but for studios that work within Agile development structures they will commonly use a technique called "story points." Instead of hours or days, a task is given a number of story points which will either reflect the perceived length of a task or its complexity. For example, a short, simple task may be 1 story point, a large but predictable task may be given 3 story points, and a small but unpredictable and complex task may be given 5 story points. This approach can work very well for Agile teams as it enables a simple, objective measure of "yesterday's weather" when planning a new sprint, and it frees developers from the perception of "being late" as 4 points does not mean "4 days" or any other time frame. However, I find that story points don't quite fit larger, more waterfall structures where deadlines are agreed in advance, as they aren't helpful with long-term scope management.

JOANNA JAKUBOWSKA, UI/UX DESIGNER

Story points are valuable ways of estimating risk, volume, effort, and complexity. They provide an excellent counterbalance and add more nuance to hourly estimations; sometimes, they help discover hidden work areas. A task in the backlog with the exact time estimation might have different story points, and this information is crucial when planning the sprint.

The best story point estimations come from different individuals/ departments with diverse perspectives. This inclusivity ensures that all voices are heard and valued in the sprint planning. Ideally, estimations should be discussed together when everyone provides reasoning for assigning a specific value. The most engaging way of doing this is "poker planning," when each team member mentally estimates after a brief discussion of the work involved. Then, everyone holds up a card with the number that reflects their estimate. If everyone agrees, great! If not, the team briefly discusses the tasks and differences and then re-estimates.

When estimating with my team, after a while, we build a shared understanding of the story points' values. For new joiners or when switching teams, the number might seem too abstract or different, but knowing the history of the project, the tech, and the team's weak and strong points can help contextualize those values better. For example, in one of my teams, the design department was small and responsible for creating pitching proposals and, therefore, for future work for the whole studio. Since the design department was spread across different projects with dynamic priorities, the waiting times for feedback and iteration would be more significant. Therefore, specific tasks had a higher risk. Other factors that could influence the values were the need for client approval, new technology that needs to be researched, dependency on other studios, the volume of work, and sometimes simply uncertainty of the work involved.

If the story points are too high, the task might need to be broken down into smaller pieces or require additional prep tasks. The story points also help create a balanced sprint plan. The team can tell if the plan is too risky or too packed at a glance. After a team delivers the estimations, it is not uncommon to reorder and reprioritize the backlog.

It is important to remember that story points are, in the end, only ESTIMATIONS. Those can change as the work evolves. All estimations require practice and team reflection. This reflection is a crucial part of the process, making each team member feel involved and responsible for the accuracy of estimations.

CLARITY AND TRANSPARENCY

One of the main reasons a producer is hired is because development is no longer as smooth as it used to be, and people are no longer sure what is happening. What they want that producer to bring is *clarity*, and it is an extremely powerful tool in untangling chaotic development.

The power of clarity

Imagine you want a group of people to all meet up for a picnic on a nearby hill. If you tell them just to "start going" they will hesitate, and they will start asking pesky questions such as "Where are we going," "When do we need to be there?" or "What will we be doing there?" This is the situation of a team that does not have clear goals, clear expectations, and clear deadlines. Whenever you are hearing people asking questions about the project, or complaining that they don't know what's going on, you can solve that problem by exposing the information in a better way. Maybe you need to regularly email the next milestone goals and deadlines, or maybe deliverable expectations need clearer documentation. They are entitled to this information and can work more efficiently if it is easy to find.

Enable decisions from everyone

Going back to our picnic metaphor, the clearer the plan, the better the decisions people will make. If you're clear that it's a picnic in the park for a few hours on the coming Saturday from midday onward, everyone will now be able to make their own decisions about food, drink, clothing, suncream, blankets, arrival times, and so on. Because the expectations, high-level needs and information have been clear, the decision-making can now be autonomous. This reflects clearly in game development; the clearer you can make the goals relating to feature content, standards, time constraints, ownership, and pipelines, then the more autonomous individuals can be.

Transparency

If you can be transparent about the purpose of your decisions, then everyone can engage with that purpose, and even solve problems in pursuit of it.

For example, if you tell someone "we need to cut half of the structures in the level" but say why, then you don't give them an opportunity to provide a solution. If, however, you explain that the level's memory budget is being exceeded, the developer may be able to advise on other actions (e.g., simplifying the structures, optimizing the furniture assets, and reducing reflective surfaces), which solves the problem without even cutting anything. Clarity and transparency empowers people to help you.

Prevent "detective work"

I have seen so much development time lost because the developers are having to "play detective," and go scrabbling around in emails, documents, and asking people just to get the basic information on what's happening. Wherever I have seen this I will generally take their question and go chasing for the answers myself so that they can go back to development, then set up a process to keep them informed. Clear communication saves time and money.

TEAM CULTURE

The culture of your team is defined by what they will do naturally. I have seen many (frankly cringe-worthy) attempts in the past by leadership teams to dictate a team's culture after executive discussions behind closed doors, presenting team values on slides with business justifications and goals. Maybe you can share aspirations this way, but your true team culture develops organically, chaotically, and is to be *observed* rather than specified.

As a producer, it's valuable to learn your team culture, as it will help you motivate, communicate, and organize the team more effectively. Here are some aspects of team culture you can study:

How do they communicate?

I have been on teams where everything is said in emails, others by Slack channels, others by group DMs, and others will call for everything. Knowing this will help you meet the team where they're at.

What values do they respect?

Talking to the people on my teams it has been interesting to hear how they will criticize and compliment each other; they will talk about each other's quality of code, quality of art, communication style, friendliness, humor, pro-activity, past experience, and more. Listen carefully to the way they talk about each other, it tells you a lot about their values.

What drives them?

Some game developers are in it to make money, others want to push the innovation of the industry, while many are far more excited about creating their own best work, or crave winning awards. Learn why your team still comes to work every day, and you can appeal to these drives when you want to motivate them, or persuade them of a decision. I'm very much motivated by having stable processes, but I know that many developers are indifferent to this notion and are far better persuaded by appealing to product quality.

What drains them?

Different people are drained by different things. I had one developer who suffered in silence for months before he finally confessed to me that he found large group video calls to be very stressful, and could work so much easier if we had individual calls instead. I was really glad when he finally told me, as I could now work with him in a way that was more efficient for me, and much more pleasant for him, and left him with much more energy for the rest of his very demanding role. Try to learn these things about your various team members, as it will empower you to build the best environment for them to work happily and efficiently.

Who's *really* in charge?

I have seen teams where everyone does what brand says, others where design calls the shots, others still which are engineering-led, and some where production controls everything. Understanding this is valuable as it will key you into the wider culture of authority, which you will often need to appeal to if you want to create any change. In some cases, it will just be one or two directors who are the ultimate authority on everything, and understanding this dynamic will allow you to avoid mistakes that make your colleagues feel exposed to the people that intimidate them.

Can I *change* a team's culture?

You can indeed. In my experience cultures grow into the spaces they inhabit, so if you want to enable a new cultural element, you have to create the space for it. Maybe your workaholic team needs to relax more, in which case creating relaxation spaces will enable a more relaxed culture to grow. At Creative Assembly we had two buildings, one of which had a kitchen with ping-pong, a pool table, and a pile of board games, while the other building's kitchen just had a few basic tables. This made such a difference to the working cultures as, in one building, you would see high-ranking staff playing ping-pong, which set an example for taking a break, and so people would take healthy breaks, while in the other building breaks were rarer, shorter, and more functional, as there was no real encouragement to spend time in the space.

Also keep in mind that it's very easy to *kill* part of a team's culture if you *take away* that space. Game Designer Jesse Schell tells a story of how a team accidentally killed their nice, social "coffee time" culture by replacing the slow coffee urn with a modern, faster coffee machine, removing the ritual in which all the chit-chat happened.[2]

Team culture analysis tools

There are many tools and services out there to help companies survey their teams and get a better picture of how their team members are motivated. A famous example is the Myers & Briggs Foundation, which quantifies various cognitive elements to build a model of the person's personality. Another example is the Management Drives consultancy, which offers a model based on motivating versus draining factors when making decisions. These forms of training and surveys can help people develop by giving them a structure for thinking about what drives them and what drains them, as well as recognizing how this can differ in other people. The easiest window into all this is to have a go yourself with the free personality test on 16personalities.com.

CHANGE AND EDUCATION

Producers are often involved with managing changes on game teams. These changes can be process changes, technology changes, team reorganizations, or anything else. Change can create stress and uncertainty in your teams if not properly managed, and can damage morale and team stability. Here are a few steps you can take to help mitigate these risks:

Communicate the purpose of the change

There is a legendary TED talk by author Simon Sinek entitled "Start With Why" and it is excellent viewing for this situation.[3] The shorthand is that inspiring change is always best done when the purpose is laid out first. In your case, make it clear what problem you are trying to solve, or what goal you are hoping to achieve with this change, and you will have a better chance of gaining your team's investment.

Refer to the change as an experiment (because it is!)

It would be disingenuous to claim that you know exactly what's going to happen when you change something, so it pays to be transparent with your team. It also allows in people's minds the idea that, if the change doesn't work, it will be rolled back to the normal if it needs to be. This can make it feel a bit less like a change being made without thought and consideration.

Communicate the plan as many times as you need to

Share up a clear plan of how the change is going to be rolled out; when each action is going to be taken, what the temporary impacts will be, and when it will all be completed. Ideally communicate this verbally in meetings, written in messages, and visually in a presented visual schedule. Make it as hard as possible for people to *not* know what's happening.

Communicate responsibilities

One of the biggest questions in people's heads when they hear that something is changing will be "Do I have to do anything?" Take the uncertainty out, and make it very clear who will be taking which actions, and if there are new expectations on the wider team, make those clear as well.

Invite feedback before and after

Once you have laid out a change plan you should invite feedback from the staff involved. They may spot key issues with your plan, and you should be prepared to adjust your plan accordingly. Ideally you want to only proceed once the team's anxieties have been addressed, and they are comfortable with the idea. Then, when the change has been completed, take the time to check in with them to see how they are finding the changed environment, and gather any fresh feedback.

Measure the outcomes

It's easy to assume that the changes we make will probably do what we expect, and confirmation bias can trick us into assuming it's worked because, well... it was *our* idea, so of course it would work! This is why you should measure against your original purpose for the change, and validate its success rationally, and share your results with your peers for them to critique. If the problem still is not solved, then you may need to take corrective action quickly.

Be prepared to roll it back, and take responsibility for the impacts

In some cases your change may do worse than nothing, and actually cause more problems for the team. A shift to a new tool may have broken all the communication pipelines people were relying on, and now everyone is lost. In these cases, it's essential to be able to instruct the team to go back to how they were working before, and facilitate this rollback. As the author of the change, you should take responsibility for the misstep and ensure no one else on the team is feeling blamed. Then it will be time to analyze what went wrong, and consider a revised approach.

FOLLOWING UP

An assumption I take to work with me every day is this: everyone is busy, and busy people forget things, lose track, and get distracted. With this in mind, it is often necessary for the producer to take on the mantle of *being annoying*, and chasing people up about the things that they are expected to be doing:

Follow up on tasks

Naturally, you should be following up on the tasks that your team has been assigned. In particular, if you can see that some tasks haven't been updated in a couple of days, then chase up the developer. Maybe they're doing the work, but just haven't updated their task-tracking. Maybe they didn't even realize the task was assigned to them, or they use a to-do list filter that was excluding that task for some reason. It could also turn out that their task is coming in late, and you now need to communicate this delay to another team with dependencies on it.

Follow up on decisions made

Again, it's very easy to assume that everyone will do what they said they would do, but you will still need to chase them up. It can be daunting chasing up more senior and director-level staff, but as a producer your job is to ensure company function, so there's no shame in hassling the higher-ups. I, for example, am a forgetful, easy-distracted person, and I don't expect this to magically improve as I go through my career, so even if I'm the most senior person in the company I will still appreciate being reminded of my promises.

Get your tools to help you

Wherever possible I get my tools to reach out to me if something is wrong. I use Jira filter subscriptions to alert me if a task hasn't been updated in more than three days. I also set reminders for chasing up actions or decisions. We have so much software designed to remind us of our commitments, so we should be leaning into it, rather than putting more cognitive load on our own memories.

MISCELLANEOUS RESPONSIBILITIES (I'M SERIOUS)

If there is a random job that is needed to keep the project running, then it will come to production, and to you. If a lot of the team are staying late, it will be the producer on the phone ordering 30 pizzas. If an executive is coming to visit the studio at short notice, the producer will book their taxi and prepare a hot-desk for them to occupy. If the motion-capture team suddenly needs a bicycle, it'll be the producer asking the cyclists on the team very nicely if they can lend their wheels for the day. You'll set up equipment for presentations, arrange furniture and equipment for in-studio focus testing, distribute company merchandise, and so on. The overall job of a producer is to "make it happen," whatever "it" happens to be.

REFERENCES

1. Manage by Exception [Internet]. Prince2.wiki. [cited 2024 Oct 8]. Available from: https://prince2.wiki/principles/manage-by-exception/
2. Jesse Schell, GDC. Game studio management: Making it great [Internet]. Youtube; [cited 2024 Oct 8]. Available from: https://www.youtube.com/watch?v=-zRaFJHK0S4
3. Talks T. Start with why—How great leaders inspire action I Simon Sinek I TEDxPugetSound [Internet]. Youtube; [cited 2024 Oct 8]. Available from: https://www.youtube.com/watch?v=u4ZoJKF_VuA

Make it happen
Producer methods

8

Alright, now that I've heaped a ton of responsibilities onto you, it's only fair I explain how I expect a producer to get all of this done. This next chapter will go through all the various methods that a producer employs to gather information, facilitate decision-making, and build a deliberate and measured environment in which a team can develop their games.

DO THE READING – COMMON PROJECT MANAGEMENT METHODOLOGIES

There are several project management methodologies that are often employed in video game development. In my experience most game companies don't strictly adhere to one or the other, but combine concepts and ideas to suit their project. Here is a very, *very* high level summary of the most commonly used methodologies:

Waterfall

The Waterfall methodology is best represented by a Gantt chart, as shown in the previous chapter. The project is planned out from start to finish with each feature broken down into its sequential, dependent components and tasks and, when visualized, it looks like a downward slope, hence the name. Waterfall is mostly applicable to projects where the end date and goals are specified at the beginning, and there are long chains of dependencies to accommodate. It allows for the long-term impacts of current problems to be quickly highlighted.

DOI: 10.1201/9781003519065-8

PRINCE2

PRINCE2 (which stands for "PRojects IN Controlled Environments 2") is a complex but powerful set of principles that can guide a project manager to creating a carefully controlled, managed environment where quality product is prioritized, and the business case kept front-and-center. Less commonly applied to video games than the other methodologies here, the ideas can be extremely effective, particularly on larger projects.

Much of the PRINCE2 approach relates to a thorough system of questions to ask about your project, in order to prevent key elements being forgotten. As an example, these are the seven "themes" of a PRINCE2 project:

- The Business Case – Why start the project?
- The Organization – Who is the team?
- The Quality – What is the product's success criteria?
- The Plans – How do we go about this?
- The Risk – Is anything uncertain?
- The Change – How can we adjust course later on?
- The Progress – Who reports? When?

The principles and processes of PRINCE2 can be very effective at keeping a complex project under control and can be very empowering for a new producer. The best place to start this research is https://prince2.wiki/.

Agile methodologies

You will see the word "Agile" on almost every producer job listing. Agile is a formalized set of development principles designed to bring flexibility to a development process by focusing on fast product iterations, regular reviews, and continuous improvement in both the product and the team's processes. This development approach requires small, self-organizing teams to function as intended. Agile has become extremely popular in the games industry, as it promises opportunities to change direction, and is particularly effective in the development of live mobile games, in which faster iterations are more likely to be possible. I advise starting your Agile research by reading the "Agile Manifesto," which you can find on https://www.agilealliance.org/.

There are several methodologies which have grown out of Agile which have seen popularity in game development. Here are some of them:

Agile – Lean

Coined at the Toyota car company, lean management advises focusing on establishing team systems and processes that create value in the product over time. Lean managers will regularly assess their processes and team functions, and look for opportunities to reduce any that create barriers to team efficiency, or cannot be justified as creating value in the product, thus being wasteful. They will also look for any opportunities to empower their employees to be individually efficient, adding to the overall efficiency of the team and system.

I would argue that lean management principles are worth applying to every project environment, as reduction of wasteful processes and improved efficiency will always benefit your teams, and the principles can easily be combined with other methodologies.

Agile – Kanban

The "Kanban" method is derived from lean methodology; this involves creating a shared backlog task that the team members each pick from when they are done with their current task. These tasks are grouped clearly into statuses of "To Do," "In Progress," and "Done." Kanban also advises identifying the maximum bandwidth of tasks a team member can own, to prevent them overloading themselves with work, which often damages efficiency. Kanban managers can measure the turnover of this system to discern the velocity of their team and enable strategic decision-making.

Agile – SCRUM

The SCRUM method is a highly formalized type of Agile development in which a team's development is broken up into a sequence of "sprints," which are two to four weeks in length. Each sprint starts with the team identifying the sprint goals based on stakeholder priorities and declaring the tasks/user stories that will achieve those goals during that sprint. They work through these tasks, and then the sprint ends with a review of the work, and a short retrospective to discuss and identify any improvements to their working methods.

SCRUM is particularly effective when you have small, multidisciplinary teams that need to collaborate on a succession of small features for quick releases.

Agile – Crystal

Crystal development is, by definition, less formalized than many of the other Agile offshoots. It still retains the goals of the Agile manifesto relating to efficiency, frequent quality, and continuous improvement, but Crystal differs by putting a strong focus on the team communication fluidity, empowerment, and psychological safety. The core tenet of Crystal is that the people, their talents and their natural interactions are the most valuable investment when it comes to getting good work done well.

Crystal methodology is most effective with teams that are able to be in constant communication and have the decision-making sources close at hand. Conversely, it is less applicable with teams that are separated by distance, time zones, and language barriers.

That's a lot of methodologies... but which one is best?

While these methodologies are all useful, it is important to understand each of their strengths and weaknesses. Coming from AAA games, I have often seen Agile principles applied in project environments which do not particularly suit them; on a project where the long-term goals, features, and deadlines are already decided, a lot of Agile processes just become overhead. My favorite example to illustrate this is the Jabberslythe from *Total War: Warhammer II*; a huge, many-limbed, multi-headed monster that took a whole six months just to *animate*! Obviously this won't fit into a three-week SCRUM sprint.

My advice is to study each of these methodologies and build an understanding of what each mechanic achieves. This will give you a much bigger toolbox to choose from when you have challenges to solve on your project. It will also bring you up-to-speed with a lot of the language used by other video game producers and project managers.

THE GOOD, THE BAD, AND THE UNNECESSARY – MEETINGS

As a producer you're going to be running many, *many* meetings in the course of your duties, and the difference between running a good meeting and running a bad meeting is very large indeed. Let's look at how to prepare for this major element of your work day.

What are meetings for anyway?

A meeting is a mechanism for quickly sharing information between a group of people, receiving feedback or clarifying questions, and then reaching decisions. The attendees should arrive prepared for the conversation so they can efficiently share their understanding and reach a decision. A meeting is usually run by a chairperson, and often there will be at least one person designated as note-taker.

The rise of the video call

Since the Covid-19 pandemic forced the games industry to adopt remote-working almost overnight (March of 2020 was an unbelievable time), video calls have become the primary medium for meetings in much of the game industry, rather than being an occasional exception. I went from having two hybrid calls per week on the *Total War* audio team to spending half my job in Microsoft Teams. There are several changes that have come with this shift to video calls:

- Unconstrained by meeting room sizes, video calls will often be huge, with dozens of people invited.
- Many more people are invited to meetings "just for visibility," with no expectation to contribute.
- Cloud-based documents with live collaboration have become essential.
- Many people will now be in the meeting on one screen, but be buried in work on the other, only half-listening.
- Many meetings are now automatically recorded and transcribed.
- Many remote meetings start with about 5 minutes of social chatter, taking the place of the idle chats in the office.

How meetings go bad

Bad meetings are the bane of everyone's workday. The conversation is aimless, nothing is decided, and it wasn't relevant to you in the first place. There are a few key things to look out for that make a meeting go bad:

- **No clear goal** – If you don't know what you're supposed to be achieving in the meeting, there is no way to make the decision.
- **Group unprepared** – You want to analyze part of the project together, but no one brought the necessary information.

- **Lack of focus** – People keep drifting off topic, and the conversation becomes irrelevant to half the group.
- **Dead air** – When the conversation keeps dropping into an awkward silence and no one takes charge to move it forward.
- **Technical problems** – Even before the pandemic, this was the scourge of conference calls, with several minutes spent mucking around with camera and mic settings.
- **Too early in the morning** – If your team aren't morning people, then an early morning meeting will just be a bleary-eyed waste of time.
- **"It could have been an email!"** – If a meeting is just a one-way sharing of information, then this cliché rings true. Meetings should be conversations, not lectures.

How to get it right and run a good meeting

Here is my advice for running effective meetings where the conversation keeps moving, stays relevant, and the decisions get acted upon:

- Clarify the goal of the meeting
- Have a clear agenda
- Tell people what information they'll need to bring
- Write all the above in the meeting booking
- Book it at an appropriate time for your team (use the schedule planners in your software)
- Plan who will take notes (or set them to auto-record/transcribe)
- Check with people before inviting them; this helps to make sure people are only there if it's relevant to them.
- As the host, be present. Your other messages can wait. They might be important, but *this is already important.*
- Drive the conversation. If it goes silent, move on to the next agenda point.
- Confirm the next steps at the end, verbally in the meeting and again in writing afterward.

Considerations for running remote and hybrid meetings

Now that we are all regularly leading remote and hybrid meetings, there are several new practices we must adopt in order to keep these meetings fruitful:

- Check your technical setup ahead of time.
- Get a decent mic. Don't make people struggle to hear you.
- Turn your camera on. Be seen to be listening.
- Make sure online participants are included equally in the conversation in hybrid meetings.
- In large video calls, people will work on the side. Get used to this, and start accommodating it.
- Always say the person's name before asking them a question, so they know to listen carefully to the whole thing. People can't see you looking at them.

Canceling a regular meeting

Every now and then it will be time to kill a regular meeting. Either it's served its purpose, or circumstances have shifted enough that there is nothing to talk about now. Ask the other invitees whether they still get any use out of it, whether they think it can be reduced in frequency, or meetings are expensive uses of employee time; eight people in a 1-hour meeting is an 8-hour cost, so make sure it's worth it.

The open channel

Many small teams wanting frequent ad hoc communication will open an online call at the beginning of the day and stay there, cameras off, and simply speak their questions aloud when they have them. This practice is reminiscent of online gaming culture where it is common to have an open voice channel with your friends while you play, and is particularly popular among coders who tend to have long periods of focused work interspersed with short, ad hoc moments of collaboration.

"Zoom fatigue"

I feel bad for the company that makes Zoom. They carried most of the world's social and business communication during a global pandemic, and now there's a medical condition named after their platform. "Zoom fatigue" is a profound feeling of being tired and drained after spending a lot of time on video calls, which require more active focus to stay engaged in than a real-life meeting, and lack the connection of nonverbal cues, body language, and – when the camera is off – even facial expressions. Another problem with constant online meetings is that so many people are multitasking through them; they will be half-listening to a meeting, working on a document, and firing messages back and forth all at once. This constant stress of the attention span is intensely draining, and I recommend closing the work windows while in online meetings.

WHO DECIDES? – GETTING DECISIONS MADE

Sometimes it feels like it's impossible to get a decision made. Others, the decision is made, but it doesn't seem to get actioned. People can even have meeting after meeting without decisions being made, and their minds boggle as to why.

Making a decision requires the following:

A. A goal
B. Data/information
C. Expertise
D. The means to action
E. The authority to action

If these are not owned by the same person/team, then your decision-making can fall apart. Imagine there are five people in a car, each separately owning one of the above faculties:

- Person A knows the destination (the goal)
- Person B has the map (the data)
- Person C knows how to drive (the expertise)
- Person D is *in the driver's seat* (the means to action)
- Person E has to approve every driving action (the authority)

This is obviously a ludicrous setup, and a recipe for going nowhere fast, but you can quite easily apply this model to game development. Imagine you are a narrative designer and you want – for example – a combat encounter with a bear in your mission. You have a goal (A), but you need the following:

- B – Project cost data from the producers for the design, concept art, character art, animation, and audio teams

- C – Expertise from the combat designer, character art lead, animation lead, and audio lead
- D – Action from the design, concept art, character art, animation, and audio leads and producers
- E – Approval from the game director and the lead producer on missions

To get this decision actioned, you now need contributions from 12 different people, which will take a lot of time and organization. The production team should observe these challenges and structure their teams in a way that the decision-making faculties for a feature can be kept in one place. Sometimes that structure will be multidisciplinary "pods," other times it will be large teams with a single, directing lead. It's a perpetual challenge, but a key part in making teams efficient.

WHO'S RESPONSIBLE FOR THIS? – THE RASCI DOCUMENT

When roles are not clearly defined, it can be very difficult to get decisions made and actioned. Because of this, many companies will set up a "RASCI" document (an acronym of Responsible, Accountable, Supporting, Consulted, and Informed), which is a document detailing each area of the project, and which team/person has a role in managing it. Here are the definitions of the roles:

- **Responsible** – The person/people doing the work (e.g., the programmers)
- **Accountable** – The individual expected to ensure the work is done (e.g., the lead)
- **Supporting** – People expected to provide support (e.g., QA, producers)
- **Consulted** – People expected to provide expertise/authority (e.g., legal team)
- **Informed** – Stakeholders that have no action required (e.g., other feature teams)

Having a RASCI document can help cement a good accountability culture in your team, clarify any uncertainties over expectations, and reduce the time it takes to get decisions made and carried out. Every few months the RASCI should be reviewed to ensure it is in line with the reality of the team culture.

WHEN DID WE DECIDE THAT? – DECISION LOGS

Video game projects can be long, and human memories can be short, so it's reasonable to assume that people will forget many of the decisions that they have made. Even if not, a decision may be questioned in retrospect by a stakeholder, and you will want to ensure you have the receipts for these decisions; it doesn't look good when your answer to "Why was this done?" is "I don't know."

To handle this, you should track any major decisions in a "decision log," including these details about each one you list:

- **Decision ID** – A unique numeric ID (e.g., "Decision 01")
- **Date** – When the decision was made
- **Event** – The event during which the decision was made, such as "weekly leads meeting," "director playtest," or "ad hoc"
- **Summary** – A single line that explains the decision (e.g., "Cut river troll from main release")
- **Rationale** – A longer description of the decision, explaining the context and the reasoning behind the decision
- **Impacts** – Clearly identify the impacts, such as "Alpha deadline now achievable," or "3 days additional programming work for person X"
- **Decision-makers** – Name the people who contributed to making the decision, including any consulted team members
- **Informed** – List any people that could be impacted by the decision and thus need to be informed (producer ensures this)
- **Related info** – Any links or documents that were part of making the decision. This could include the meeting notes, bug reports, or the dataset that informed the decision.

And yes, it's the producer's job to ensure that a decision log is updated and usable. I advise checking for new decisions each week, and including the updates in any weekly reports you make. The decision log can also be useful when reviewing the RASCI document, as it shows the empirical truth of how your team makes decisions.

WHAT'S THE WORST THAT CAN HAPPEN? – RISK REGISTERS

A key responsibility of producers is to study and mitigate the risks on the project. The PRINCE2 methodology insists upon maintaining a detailed "risk register" to help with managing and mitigating the risks relating to your team and your project. Generally this will be in the form of a table or a spreadsheet.

The exact columns in a risk register can vary, but this is what I am used to:

- **Risk ID** – A unique numeric ID (e.g., "Risk 01")
- **Date** – When the risk was logged
- **Category** – The affected area (e.g., performance).
- **Summary** – A short line identifying the risk
- **Status** – The status of the risk (i.e., current issue, potential issue, mitigated issue)
- **Description** – A long description to detail the risk detailing the causes, effects, and consequences
- **Likelihood** – e.g., high, medium, or low
- **Impact** – e.g., high, medium, or low
- **Priority** – A score referencing the **likelihood** and **impact** to help the team focus on the worst risks first
- **Mitigation** – The actions being taken
- **Owner** – The person accountable for the mitigation
- **Updates** – Any notable changes to the context of the risk

Any updates to these risks should be included in your regular reports, and the register regularly reviewed and maintained. A note on accessibility: Some teams use the traffic light colors of red, amber, and green, respectively, to communicate their risk statuses. However as a color-blind producer, I politely ask you to please include the *words* as well as any colors in your reporting. Thank you.

IDENTIFY, SOLVE, PREVENT – A PROBLEM-SOLVING METHOD

All producers are problem-solvers by trade, and these problems can be almost anything, ranging from the technical, to the logistical, to the social. With this in mind it is good to build a personal discipline of problem-solving so that you can efficiently deal with every challenge that comes your way.

Here is a model that I use when solving a problem. It comes in three parts:

Step 1 – Identify the problem

First step is to analyze the problem, which begins with observing the **impacts**. As an example, the **impact** you observe is that the build crashes whenever entering the main menu (a lush forest glade), specifically an out-of-memory crash, meaning that no one can test the game (another **impact**).

Next you look for the **causes** of the issue which, after scouring through check-in records and the main menu virtual scene, you identify to be an increase in the number of trees in the scene, which is using up all the memory when the menu scene loads.

You can break this **cause** into a number of **contributing factors**, which in this case are:

- the memory budget of the scene
- the number of trees in the scene
- the individual memory cost of each tree.

Great, you have identified the problem.

Step 2 – Solve the immediate problem

The first thing to do is to address the **impacts** immediately, that is, stop the build crashing and allow the team to test again. You discuss the **contributing factors** with a few developers, and together you solve the immediate problem by optimizing the tree model so that the memory budget is no longer exceeded by the current number. Build no longer crashes. Problem solved. Great.

Step 3 – Prevent the problem recurring

However, you're not done. It's a real problem when the team can't test the game, so you want to prevent the problem from happening again, which means addressing the initial **cause**. In this case, the initial **cause** is one or more artists adding more trees than the memory budget can support, so this is what you have to prevent. Together with the team you implement a warning system in the editor to prevent additional models if the memory budget will be exceeded.

With a preventative process in place you should monitor for any relapse, as well as recording the events in the risk register, and any key decisions in the decision log.

GRAND DESIGNS – PIPELINES AND PROCESSES

Production is not just admin; there is a great deal of creativity that goes into creating a functioning team of people, and this is well-illustrated by the designing of pipelines and processes. Here are some thoughts to get your brain going:

What is a designed process?

A designed process is an established set of actions for handling a situation, event, or occurrence. For example, a common process in game development is a tester discovering a bug:

1. Encounter bug in game
2. Check database to see whether it's been reported
   a. If not, report it
3. Resume testing

As a producer, you should consider designing a process whenever you expect a situation to come up repeatedly. Onboarding lots of people? Design a process. Outsourcing sound effects again? Design another one. Directors want a weekly show-and-tell from the whole team? Yep. Process. Processes remove the stress of figuring out what needs doing each time something happens, and speeds up the reaction time.

What is a pipeline?

A pipeline is a collection of processes and people that simplify meeting a regular need. An everyday example of a pipeline is ordering a sandwich in a shop like Subway. They slice the bread, add the meat, add the cheese, add the salad, drizzle the sauce, then toast it, slice it, wrap it, and give it to you, all while moving down the counter from section to section.

Game-development teams have many pipelines to match their repeated needs: art assets, audio assets, build delivery, translation, legal reviews, and so on. Any time you see repeated requirements in your role, you may be able to streamline them with a pipeline. Remember, any pipeline you develop should be clearly documented and presented to the team, so they can be educated in its use.

Automation

The best pipelines are ideally ones you completely encapsulate in software, and more and more technology is being developed to easily enable the automation of day-to-day team processes. The Slack messaging tool has its Workflow Builder, with which you can easily build automated communication pipelines. Microsoft also has Power Automate, which you can use to create automated information pipelines between Microsoft Office products such as Teams, Outlook, and Excel. Take advantage of all of these and speed up your pipelines and processes.

The right thing to do should be the *easiest* thing to do

When I was young it was so incredibly easy to pirate music that it became normal among my peers. We eventually stopped, but not out of respect for the law, but because Apple iTunes and other mp3 stores appeared, *which made buying easier than stealing.*

This is a lesson you should apply to your process design. If you want to change the way people do something, you will have to ensure that it is the easiest option for them. If they have to fill in a complicated form or learn a strange new tool, then it will probably fail, as people will either just stick to the old way or stop entirely. However, if your form makes it easy to get information right, auto-fills information, and does the rest at the click of a button, then people will pick it up and be glad for the simplification.

On the subject of design...

I think design is an underappreciated skill in the field of production, so I will recommend you invest in it. Producers design processes, pipelines, reports, documentation, tools, and team structures. You can do worse than to start with the book *The Design of Everyday Things* by Donald Norman, which will give you an excellent introduction to how simple design choices can change how people interact with the world. I also recommend having a play with https://machinations.io/, which is a quality tool for designing and simulating systems and processes.

OUTSOURCING – EFFECTIVE, BUT NOT SIMPLE

Another common example of a pipeline that you may need to design is the outsourcing pipeline. As internet connections have improved, more and more outsourcing studios have sprung up around the world, enabling huge and highly responsive content factories, and often at competitive prices.

While outsourcing can sound like a magic bullet for a development challenge, it is very common for outsourcing to go wrong, with money burned on sub-par content that needs extensive rework or to be thrown away entirely. There are a lot of things a producer can do to ensure a smooth and effective pipeline, so let's explore them.

Why outsource at all?

The right time to outsource is when you want a large but *temporary* increase in output velocity for a specific part of your project. This is why 2D art, 3D models, and translations are quite common targets for outsourcing, as they are only needed at one part of the project. If you have three-year long projects, you likely wouldn't hire your own translators, as they would have no work to do for about 2.5 years. However, if you are a live game with constant translation needs, then the criteria of "temporary velocity increase" is no longer met, and you should consider hiring a translator full-time.

Which work is good for outsourcing?

When considering outsourcing for your projects, you want to identify easily outsourced content, which I see as falling into the following criteria:

- **Small units** – Allows the outsourcer to efficiently distribute the work among their team
- **Simple** – Creates fewer questions and less communication overhead
- **Self-contained** – Reduces dependencies and makes for easier scheduling

- **Generic** – Requires less direction from your team
- **Aligned with the outsourcer's skillset** – Don't go to a 2D specialist for 3D art. Find the right team for your needs.

How does it go wrong?

Of course, it is common for much of this to go wrong, in many ways:

- **Bad choice of work** – Choosing work that is large, complex, or unprecedented tends to result in slow work that needs constant direction or rework
- **Bad pipeline** – If your asset transfer and implementation pipelines are manual or error-prone, then getting every piece of work back from the outsourcer becomes a nightmare.
- **Communication not fluid** – Priorities falling out of sync, direction going in ways, problems going unreported. All could have been solved with regular communication.
- **Distrust and blame** – When things go wrong people naturally get defensive of their own team, and this often pushes blame onto the outsourcer, leading to tense conversations, damaged relationships, and micro-management.
- **Dysfunctional partner** – Sometimes you can do everything right, but your supplier simply has too many internal issues to be effective, and the relationship needs to be terminated.

How do I get it right?

OK, enough of how it can go wrong. Here is my advice for setting yourself up for success with outsourcing:

- **Talk to IT first** – IT staff (rightly) dislike urgent messages to give random companies access to your source code. Ask in advance for their collaboration in setting up your outsourcers and pipelines in a secure way.
- **Select the right work** – Keep it small, simple, generic, and a good match for your outsourcer's capabilities.
- **Pick the right partner** – Study their portfolio, ask for references, and request example assets to make sure they will match your needs.
- **Establish a good relationship** – Calls are OK, but it is much better to meet them in person at least once; establishing a relationship

is far more effective in person when you can take your time and get to know each other.

- **Clear statement of work** – When writing up the contract, ensure that the statement of work has clear deadlines, deliverables, and conditions. This can avoid difficult arguments later on.
- **Good content pipeline** – Make it as easy as possible for your outsourcers to get their content to you. A shared repository in your source control is often best, so their content can go straight into your game. If this isn't possible, get the file transfer protocols and accounts set up and tested at the start.
- **Good *direction* pipeline** – Often the direction will need to come from other members of your team, so ensure that all work requests are accompanied with the necessary direction to complete it correctly.
- **Support them throughout** – Ensure there is a point of contact for the outsourcer (often you) to request help with direction, technical issues, and anything else they need.
- **Pay them on time** – Outsourcers talk, and the reputation of your business as a co-development partner will travel. If your business builds a reputation for never paying on time, outsourcers may avoid you, decreasing your partner market. Pay them on time, and build a good reputation.
- **Document the pipeline immediately** – Ideally, write the documentation for your outsourcing pipeline *as you set it up*, so you can easily share the knowledge required to run the pipeline correctly and effectively.

With game development spreading around the world more and more, and the difference in development costs from west to east becoming so pronounced, I fully expect remote outsourcing to increase, so be ready to ace it.

REPORTS THAT SERVE YOUR BOSS (AND YOU!)

Reports are going to be another one of your main responsibilities as a producer, particularly on larger teams. You could be reporting on feature progress, budget expenditure, bugs, reviews, team activities, and so on. As well as writing reports when requested by the team, I also personally use them as a self-management technique; whatever I have to put in a weekly report becomes information that I definitely see each week.

Similar to the processes and pipelines, it is worth engaging your inner designer when writing reports to ensure that they are effective communication tools. Here is a guide you can use to help map out the needs of your report:

Identify the questions that the report needs to answer

It's very easy to write a big noisy report with tons of data, numbers, metrics, and charts, and it still proves useless because the initial questions hadn't been identified. To help you figure these out, I have seen variants of these core questions almost always come up:

- What has happened recently?
- What's happening now?
- What's happening soon?
- Are we on track?
- Do I, the reader, need to do anything?

You should figure out the answer to these questions in your report's context, and design the report to answer them.

Identify any information that you need to revisit each week

This is where you can make your reports into tools of self-empowerment. Let's say you are the producer for a tech art team, you might want to always know the average frame rate of each level. Adding this to the report means that you will now have an accountable routine to check and log this each week. This is do-able for anything you want to keep up with; upcoming team holidays, bug numbers, office events, and so on.

Design a report that people will read

If you think of a newspaper as a report, this will give you an idea of how important the placement of information can be. Every paper will have the **Headline** (aka the bit everybody reads), the **Story** (aka the bit *some* people read), and the **Data** (all the trade, financial and business information in the back pages) that most people ignore, but are very important to a few key people. You can use this to inspire your report structure:

- **The headline**
  - Answers the question "Are we on track?"
  - Answers the question "Do I, the reader, need to do anything?"
  - Short lines on the most important takeaways from the report
  - Status of any key work items
- **The story**
  - Answers the questions about what's happening then/now/soon
  - Shows a representation of the team's recent, current, and upcoming activity
  - Include updates to risk and decisions
- **The data**
  - The info on which your answers are based (e.g., tasks, bugs, budget spend, etc.)
  - This can back up your conclusions in case you are challenged on them, which often happens if it's bad news.
  - Sharing the data every week builds trust in your headline and story.
- **Quick links**
  - A weekly report is a good place to centralize any useful links relating to your team (e.g., roadmaps, wikis, holiday trackers, etc.)

SAY WHAT? – TEAM LANGUAGE AND NAMING CONVENTIONS

There were genuinely times when I was working at FundamentalVR when I had to DM the PO, CSM, and QA because the DLT raised in the SOS that the SLT had read in the MMO about a KOL asking about the ETA of the POC… and everyone knew what this meant. Similarly, there were times at Creative Assembly where I would be arranging audio tasks for authoring and implementation of launches, flybys, impacts, foley, solo movement, group movement, 2D ambiences, 3D ambiences, 5.1 stems, and stereo mix-downs…and everyone knew what *that* meant.

Every team develops its own language organically, so sometimes it's worth putting in the effort to ensure that the *shared* language has enough consistent elements that the teams can work together.

Keep a team glossary

You should ensure that there exists a glossary of terms that anyone can contribute to, and start logging all the various names, acronyms, and assorted jargon that your team uses on a regular basis. Make sure this can be easily searched, and have it linked in your onboarding documentation so your new starters can get up to speed with your team's unique lingo quickly. To get you started, there will be a glossary of common game production terms at the back of this book.

Naming conventions

If you are working with technical teams, you should champion having good naming conventions in your game systems. After getting frustrated with the chaotic naming of the audio assets used in *Alien: Isolation,* the audio team spent time crafting a robust naming convention for all their audio assets, so they could build technical information into each filename (e.g., bit-rate, channels, loop, or one-shot), which made developing the *Halo Wars 2* sound, music, and dialogue much smoother and less error-prone.

You will probably be involved with naming conventions at one time or another. Here are some examples of where I have seen formal naming conventions help development:

- Task summaries
- Bug summaries
- Art assets
- Audio assets
- Text string IDs
- IT support tickets

LOOK BOTH WAYS – PROJECT DATA

Producers will have to deal with a lot of different kinds of data throughout their career, so learning how to handle and present data will be a valuable investment.

Types of data

Just to scare you, here are just some of the types of data that you may need to handle as a producer:

- Budgets – money
- Budgets – staff days
- Task estimated time
- Task actual time
- Team task velocity
- Bug numbers
- Team bug-fixing velocity
- Sales figures
- User figures

Don't worry. They won't all land on your plate at once.

Burndown charts

While all the above are potentially relevant in your career, the initial focus is likely to be on your teams' tasks progress, so you are likely to be dealing with "burndown" charts. Here is an example below of a sprint burndown chart for a two-week sprint, starting on a Thursday and finishing on a Wednesday (Figure 8.1):

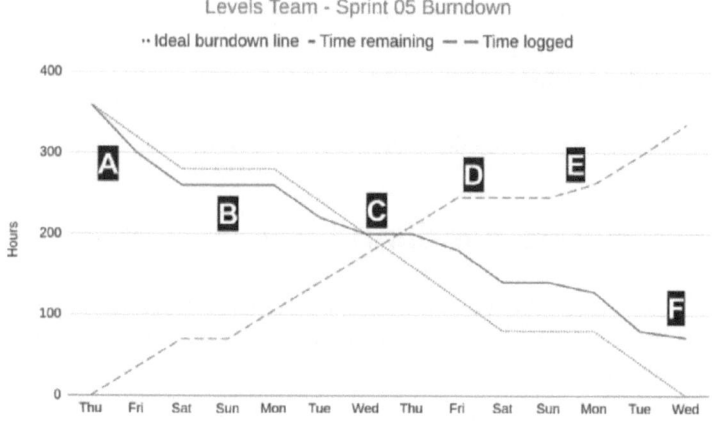

FIGURE 8.1   An example of a burndown chart.

This chart is measured in hours and shows three data trends:

- **Ideal burndown line (dotted)** – This is an artificial line, designed to show how the "Time remaining" line should ideal look
- **Time remaining (solid)** – The total hours of work remaining each day in the assigned tasks for this two-week sprint, reduced manually by the team as they work
- **Time logged (dashed)** – The total hours manually logged by this team in their tasks each day

Burndown charts can be used to highlight when something is going wrong somewhere with the team's work velocity. I have annotated six points on the chart where observations can be made:

- **A** – The team initially burn through their tasks faster than expected
- **B** – No work is done over the weekend
- **C** – On Wednesday time is being logged but no progress is being achieved. The team may be distracted from their work, blocked by technical issues, or the tasks could simply be taking longer than expected
- **D** – No time is logged on Friday, even though work was achieved. The producer should check in and ensure they continue logging their hours.
- **E** – Some hours were logged on Sunday, suggesting someone was working overtime. The producer should check in and see whether they need support.
- **F** – The sprint ends with around 80 out of 360 hours remaining, recording a team velocity of 280 hours. Next sprint, the producer should consider only scheduling 280 hours and observing the velocity again.

There is at least one more oddity in this chart. See what you can find!

Common data handling tools

Once you are comfortable with burndown charts, you should start preparing yourself for more complex data manipulation, so it will be essential to investigate the following tools:

- **Spreadsheets**
  - The bread-and-butter of production and project management

- Can store simple tables or manipulate complex databases
- Use formulas to handle all your complex mathematics
- Insert charts to make your data look pretty
- Macros can turn hours of work into a button-click
- Example tools: Microsoft Excel, Google Sheets, Apache Calc
- **Databases**
  - Designed to handle huge reams of data
  - So large that they have a special language for searching them (SQL)
  - Can be fed into data visualizers for analysis
  - Example tools: Microsoft Access, Apache Base
- **Data visualizers**
  - Designed for presentation and analysis of databases
  - Extremely powerful information tools
  - Metrics can be displayed in a browser for easy sharing
  - Example tools: Microsoft Power BI, Google Charts

CUT THE FEATURE, SAVE THE GAME

This one can be hard, but it is essential that producers are able to make the decision to cut game content and control the scope of work. If there is no one that can make this decision, the project is not under control and is likely to head toward a nasty crunch period at the end.

Why might content need cutting?

The most obvious reason to cut content is that you don't have time. You've measured the workload and have realized that you don't have enough time to complete all the work, the deadline can't move, and additional staff are available. The only option is to cut some work and balance out the schedule again. Another reason may be that the content is just too unstable or technically complicated to safely implement.

And finally, sometimes the idea just…sucks. In my very first game jam, we spent 24 hours prototyping a physics-based game balancing a ball on two fans (my idea) only to find out that it really wasn't fun. So we threw the whole game idea away and spent the remaining 24 hours making a fun little pixel-art game with lasers instead. We cut an entire game to make space for another.

How to talk to the team about cutting features

Game developers are, by nature, extremely passionate about the games they are making and can get quite upset if a producer walks in and tells them their great idea has been thrown away for budget reasons. To help mitigate this, you should first explain the reason for cutting content (i.e., protecting them from crunch), but also make sure that it is the creative owner that chooses the cut content. The producer can bring the options, but the creative should make the choice. This is why the producer was hired.

Everything is easier with a prioritized backlog

Cutting content can be so much easier if you keep your backlog prioritized and schedule development in priority order. This way, when the clock starts running out and content needs to be cut, it's easier to start from the lowest priority content. Again, involving the team in the prioritization embeds their voice into the decision-making, which can make the cutting process less demoralizing.

If you simply run out of time, the clock decides which of your features is cut, and not you. Take action in advance to ensure the important work happens first.

SMOOTH OPERATION – HOW TO PREVENT "CRUNCH"

It is well-known that a lot of game development studios go through a period of "crunch" as they approach their deadlines. This is a long stretch of sustained overtime, rarely paid, and often with no clear goal other than "do more!" In case it isn't obvious, let me be clear; I do not approve of crunch in game development, instead I see it as a failure of production and an embarrassment to the industry. I write this chapter in the hope that the next generation of producers can proceed into the world of game development equipped to mitigate this practice, so let's investigate the problem.

What causes crunch?

Crunch happens when you need to meet a deadline, but do not reduce your scope or increase your resource, so the only available solution is to squeeze more out of your existing resources. I think of crunch as resulting from a mixture of feature creep and feature *greed*; often a team cannot face the idea of reducing the scope of the game and completing these features then takes priority over their team's work-life balance. The usual pattern is that the team spends longer on completing features than anyone planned, bulldozes through your polish time, and ends up squeezing the bug-fixing time so small as to be woefully inadequate. At this point you don't even have the option to cut features as they are now completed, but due to the lack of bug-fixing your game is a buggy, broken, unshippable mess. Now all you can do is spend the time (and overtime) desperately fixing bugs until the product will pass certification.

What is the cost of crunch?

Crunch can be devastating to your team. The long, forced hours are draining, detrimental to their health and damage their relationships both in and out of the studio. In crunch you feel like you're *always behind* and will never catch up, which is a key factor in employee burnout. Crunch is also inefficient; tired employees make more mistakes, causing more bugs, requiring *even more overtime*. Crunch also wrecks the development team's trust in both their production team and their director team, and they will blame them for poor planning and decision-making. Also, because the bug-fixing time was reduced, the game will actually ship with more bugs than if the scope had been properly managed.

How to predict crunch

There are a lot of warning signs that the production team can look out for to see that their project is not looking to come in on time. Some methods include:

- **Project data trends** – Measuring the team's velocity versus resource can show in advance whether the current scope will not make the deadline, allowing you to take action.
- **Risks not being mitigated** – If the risks you are tracking are not being mitigated, then you have a mounting stack of problems which will likely cause trouble later on.
- **Testing/bug-fixing time disappearing** – If your two months of testing and bug-fixing has shrunk to three weeks in the schedule, then you can safely assume you're not going to have time to assure your game's quality.

- **Ask the team** – I am often surprised by how good the intuition of some developers can be. Without any of the production metrics, tools, or burndowns they can still often predict when the game is going to shape up, and how bad development is going to go. Take these hunches seriously.
- **Ask QA** – Bug numbers are useful, but if you want a real state of the game, then just ask the QA team. If an experienced QA lead says the game is unshippable, you can generally take their word for it. The same goes for if they say it's great, and ready to go. Check in with QA leads regularly to know how your game is shaping up.

How to prevent crunch

You've seen the signs and can tell that disaster is looming at the next release, so now it's time to do something about it. Here is a set of tools you can use to try and reduce, or even fully prevent crunch:

- **Build multiple contingencies into schedules** – In my previous companies, we would assume a maximum work rate of 70%, only tasking 7 days of work in every 10. Similarly we would build hidden multipliers into our task-tracking tools to quietly inflate the apparent workload, tricking us into being more conservative. These contingencies create space for problems, delays, and unwelcome surprises to occur without jeopardizing your delivery date.
- **Chase up the risks** – If the risk register is going red, then get them chased up and mitigated, roping in the rest of the team to help clear the deck if necessary.
- **Reduce scope** – Easily the most effective option. Cut however many low priority features it takes to bring the scope to an achievable amount. If your team is slow, make sure to take the reduced velocity into account in your updated schedules.
- **Increase the resource** – If you have the budget, bringing on additional developers can help bring some workloads back under control. However, not all work can be worked on in parallel, so adding more people won't work. In the words of many a tech lead, "Nine programmers can't have a baby in one month."
- **Push the release date** – Many games have been saved from a disastrous launch by pushing the release date to allow more bug-fixing time.
- **Targeted, surgical overtime** – If there is a clear, achievable piece of work that will relieve a development bottleneck, then you can

discuss the potential for overtime with your team. Commonly a studio will gift each staff member doing overtime an additional day to their holiday allowance to make up for the lost free time. Remember that the other developers, IT and Ops teams may not be around to support during this overtime.

- **Halt development entirely** – I've had to do this, and I think it may be the best decision I've ever made as a producer. We'd had a rushed, disastrous release to the client; key features weren't working, bugs were everywhere, the client was furious, and we were being asked to try and cram in *even* more features as fast as possible to appease them. I decided that we needed to stop implementing, take a breath, review the product, and prioritize the fixes necessary to bring it back to a stable state. We knew our next milestone delivery would have to be reduced in scope to accommodate this, but we had to change our toxic process. A famous example of this was "Operation Health," where the team making *Tom Clancy's Rainbow Six Siege* (2015, Ubisoft Montreal) announced to the fans that the next live season would contain no new content at all, and instead the team would focus on the much needed bug-fixing and technology improvements necessary to stabilize the game and the live-development platform. A phrase I like to use when we need to slow down is "the fastest cars have the best brakes."

Is all overtime bad?

After the ranting above it may surprise you when I write this but in truth, no, I don't think all overtime is bad. Some voluntary overtime is actually quite healthy, definitely productive, and even satisfying. You will often see game developers staying late when their passion has taken over and they are "in the zone." I myself have stayed late in the office many times because I found I could get deep into some complex work when no one else was around, and it felt great because I knew it would be an investment in my own working life.

It's worth remembering that almost all game developers start out as hobbyists, effectively making games unpaid *for themselves* before they discover their first game salary. Game jams are a completely voluntary exercise in overtime, where people gather to sacrifice a weekend to make a game in 48 hours, often foregoing both sleep and healthy nutrition, and they are absolutely thrilling. Many studios will run ongoing overtime food support, either stocking their office kitchens or ordering takeaway for the team, which can sometimes make overtime feel a little more like a long game jam. I can't tell you how much Nando's I ate at Creative Assembly…

Check on your staff doing overtime, and make sure it's coming from a place of healthy passion, rather than a desperate feeling of being behind on their work.

KEEP IMPROVING – REGULAR RETROSPECTIVES

Many of the project management methodologies prescribe regular retrospectives as a way to ensure that the way your team works is continuously improving.

These don't need to be as big as an end-of-project postmortem, although the method is similar:

- Team members write sticky notes for each of these categories:
  - START – Suggestions for new practices (e.g., team playtests)
  - STOP – Any common problems (e.g., changing global settings without team discussion)
  - CONTINUE – Anything that they have been finding helpful (e.g., QA reminding developers about bugs)
- Each team member gets three votes which they place on the cards they think are the most important.
- Cards are discussed in priority order, with actions being proposed and decided upon by the team.
- The producer documents the actions, ensuring they have owners, and shares the notes with the team after the session.

This is also a good way to see how your team perceives progress; if they put "cross-team communication" in the START column one month, and then in the CONTINUE column the next month, then clearly they are perceiving improvements in that regard, of which you can take note.

READ THE MANUAL – MASTER YOUR TOOLS

Every now and then I discover a life-changing feature in a tool that I've been using for years, and kick myself that I never knew about it before.

Conversation view in Outlook changed my inbox with a click, Ctrl-Z in Slack meant I could unsend half-sent messages, and realizing that I could subscribe daily to filters in Jira was like hiring three producers just for me. Most of the day-to-day office and management tools that we use as producers are absolutely brimming with features that can accelerate you, for example, keyboard shortcuts, saved views, integrations with other software, and so on. If you want to *really* get advanced, then many of these tools have programming languages and scripting APIs built into them with which you can start automating many functions entirely. I took one course on Udemy.com for Excel Visual Basic for Applications, and this has equipped me to build extremely powerful production tools, many of which are apparently still being used in my previous studios.

I would advise training sessions for your production team on the commonly shared tools such as advanced Excel training, the SlackCertified course, or others. Get your existing experts to share their knowledge in workshops, which will upskill the team around them and build respect on the team as a whole. I understand that life is busy, and that endless learning can get fatiguing, but even if you just watch one "10 tips and tricks" video on YouTube for each of your tools, you will upgrade your performance in every one of your working functions.

Empower them
People and communication

9

In every production job advert and CV you will see a reference to "good communication skills," and with good reason. Producers should aspire to be the experts in communication at their studios, which will not only help them do their best job but set an example to the other developers, and uplift the communication skills of the whole team. This chapter will break down some key elements of communication in the workplace, with some practical methods for the tricky bits.

CONNECTING PEOPLE

The Covid-19 pandemic and subsequent lockdowns have clearly illustrated to the public the impacts of isolation. It is despairing, demoralizing, and completely breaks any feeling of community between people.

However, you don't need a global pandemic for people to become isolated. Many people in large companies are already disconnected from each other, meaning they can't help each other with problems, and may be too shy to ask for help when they need it. For this reason it is valuable to help keep your team connected to the community at large, and make it easy for them to find each other. Most of my time solving problems in production is simply about introducing one expert to another; it helps get the problem solved, and gives them the contacts they need to solve it in the future.

Here are some methods to help build connections in your team:

- **Social onboarding** – When a new person arrives on the team, arrange a team lunch or video call and invite everyone to talk about themselves and about life at the studio. This helps the new

DOI: 10.1201/9781003519065-9

person build lots of connections quickly in a relaxed environment and makes them feel like they're joining a community.

- **Actively introduce people** – When running a meeting make sure to introduce any new attendees before getting down to business. Use the rule "People before work." This is doubly important in remote times, as onboarding remotely to a company is very different to walking into a studio, and the chances to connect come rarely, so make them successful.
- **Have a help channel** – At FundamentalVR people were losing a lot of time asking production questions in private messages, as they would need to try multiple producers until they found the one with the answer. To improve this we set up an "Ask Production" channel in Slack and invited the whole company, in which people could ask anything they wanted. This centralized the questions, helped the answers come quicker, and reduced repeated questions because the whole company would learn from the shared answers.
- **Run social activities** – At Creative Assembly the football team was a huge driver of social connection, as was the walking club, board game club, and so on. These allowed people to really get to know each other without the pressure of work, and built an incredible community feeling.
- **Encourage social channels** – Many companies have employee-driven social channels which people connect to each other outside of working topics. Common favorites are #pets, #parents, #neurodiversity, and so on. You should also encourage channels for national groups, which help new employees from other countries get connected and settled.
- **Team Community Newsletter** – It's often hard to know what's going on in the company, especially when everyone's remote, so people may not realize the right activities for them are happening. Have a monthly community newsletter to keep the studio's social scene and contacts transparent easy to find.
- **Don't carry letters, launch satellites!** – Producers can easily end up carrying questions from person A to person B, only to find that B has clarifying questions for A, who then thinks that B is overthinking the questions and so on, creating a cycle of frustration and time wasting. Instead, I recommend "launching the satellite" which is where you permanently connect them to each other; you introduce them, set up a shared channel, or create the regular meeting they need to stay in contact. This also avoids the problem where I – a nontechnical producer – am carrying technical questions from programmer to programmer without actually understanding what I'm asking.

There's a saying derived from an old African proverb which reads "It takes a village to raise a child." The same is true for game development; in a village people feel safer and better able to handle the stresses of life because they know the people around them will support them. Do the work to make your team a "village."

DO YOU TRUST ME? – BUILDING TRUST IN PEOPLE

One of the key ingredients of a community is trust. In my experience, everyone acknowledges the value of trust, but not everyone knows exactly how it works, or how to build it. I believe producers should be experts in the management and building of trust. If you agree, then read on:

Why is trust important?

Trust is the feeling that someone will give you the support you need, when you need it, allowing for more vulnerability and honesty in your relationship. Extensive studies have shown how the psychological safety of a team enables more innovation and creative risk-taking.

By contrast, in teams where trust is lacking you start to get cultures of blame, pessimism, and dishonesty. People hoard information in case they need it later to handle a power dynamic, meaning that other members of your team are disempowered. You find that innovation completely shuts down, as people do not want to take any risks and may not even want to draw attention to themselves.

Different types of trust

Trusting someone can relate to one of several aspects of their person. Here are some different aspects of trust to consider:

- **Availability** – Will they be there if you call out for help?
- **Loyalty** – Will they back you up unconditionally?
- **Empathy** – Will they understand your problem from your perspective?
- **Reliability** – Will they keep their word and take action?
- **Capability** – Are they capable of the help they offer?

How is trust lost?

Trust can be lost in many ways, some examples being:

- **Blame** – Someone publicly blames you for a problem, when you expected them to back you up.
- **Inaction** – Maybe they promise to take action to help you, but never actually deliver on their words.
- **Dishonesty** – Perhaps someone starts hiding information from you. This can be tricky, because they might think they're protecting you, but this always comes with the risk of breaking the feeling of trust.
- **Disrespect** – Someone doesn't take you seriously, either belittling your experience or dismissing your problem as unimportant.
- **Problems** – An upstream team is always creating problems for your downstream team, and it can make them feel like "the people that always ruin your day."

Building trust in you

Before you start nurturing trust relationships on your team you will need to build their trust in you. If you can see that two team members are having problems with each other, here is where you can start:

- **Approach them individually** – Reach out to each person, and start a conversation about the problem they're having
- **Show humility and openness** – Open with your desire to help, but admit that you don't know what the true problem is yet and you'd like to understand it from their perspective.
- **Listen to their problem** – Let them talk. Keep them talking until they start running out of points to make. This will both educate you about the issue and make them feel heard and respected.
- **Acknowledge their emotions** – Whatever is going on, emotions are a real pressure that drives people and, while they can be managed, they should not be ignored or stigmatized. Tell them it's OK to be frustrated in their situation, or that you would feel anxious too, in their shoes.
- **Identify their goal** – When they've explained the problem to you, ask them what solving it would look like. You want to find out what their goal is, so you can ensure any solutions accomplish this.

- **Make them feel safe in your space** – If they feel nervous in front of you, or are worried about any kind of retribution, then they won't be honest with you. Make sure they know you're on their side.

Building trust between others

Once you've done your work with the individuals, now it's time to bring the group together: A lot of these steps are basically the same as when talking to individuals:

- **Start the conversation** – Invite them to the same meeting with the promise that everyone will be listened to.
- **Maintain the tone of humility and openness** – Keep clear that you're looking for everyone to find solutions together, and that you're not going to simply take control and start giving orders.
- **Share the problems** – Lay out everything going wrong as expressed by the team, but as objectively as possible. Keep any blame out of the conversation.
- **Acknowledge the emotions** – Again, make it clear to the group that it's OK to be frustrated, or get emotional when experiencing problems at work.
- **Share the goals** – Make clear each person's goal, as a setup to finding solutions that help everyone.
- **Highlight common goals** – Where possible, look for any common goals in what you have been told, and point them out. It can help the groups understand that they are working toward the same end, just from different perspectives.
- *This part of the conversation isn't about solving the problem, this is about getting the people to understand each other's problems, and build empathy for each other.*

Connect "being vulnerable" with the solving of problems

Hopefully you have now created an environment of openness and vulnerability, but this can still feel uncomfortable. You want to work toward finding the solutions so that people can feel the benefits of being vulnerable:

- **Invite suggestions for solutions** – Get all parties to start suggesting solutions. Ensure everyone has a chance to suggest something before picking a solution.

- **Ensure all parties have time to explain** – Make sure no one is cutting anyone else off, and if necessary step in and say "please let them finish first." This ensures everyone knows that they will be heard.
- **Support their suggested solution** – As the group starts narrowing in on the solution, support them with it, being clear how you will help it happen.
- **Commit to your actions** – This all falls down if you don't actually do anything afterward, so make sure you keep the promises you make.
- **Communicate/Celebrate the solved problem** – When a problem has actually been solved, celebrate it. It's easy to forget the solved problems. Keeping a "wins" section in your weekly reports can help with this.

Maintaining trust

After the problem is solved you will want to prevent it reoccurring, which means maintaining the trust relationship, so you should:

- **Keep the parties in regular contact** – Maybe this is a regular sync meeting, or maybe a shared Slack channel is enough. Don't let them get isolated from each other again.
- **Keep their problems and goals in view** – Ensure there is a regular forum or report where their problems and goals are highlighted. This can help ensure all parties don't feel forgotten again.
- **Maintain a transparent environment** – Keep any further discussion on the topics in full view of everyone, so that no one feels their agency is being taken away from them again. There really is very little that needs to be kept secret in a game development team.

DO YOU TRUST *THAT*? – BUILDING TRUST IN DOCUMENTATION

While we're talking about trust we need to talk about how, in many studios, the documents, wikis, and status pages are so out-of-date that no one trusts them anymore. It's time to talk about "document trust":

Why don't people trust documents?

When there are too many pages, documents, and wikis to maintain some will fall behind, get forgotten, and effectively rot as the actual information changes but the document is never corrected. As soon as anyone finds out the information is wrong, then the trust in that document is broken, and people will revert to asking a trusted *person* instead.

What problems does this cause?

Out-of-date documents generally cause people to give up on the documentation and stop reading it, leading to additional communication overhead and more detective work. Or, and this is worse, they *believe* the information and make the wrong decisions. This second consequence is likely to accelerate with the arrival of artificial intelligence (AI) tools in business communication (e.g., Microsoft Copilot). These tools are starting to look really powerful, but currently there is no way for the models to know when a document is out-of-date or not, so we can't trust the AI tools either.

What do I do about it?

The method is similar to how you maintain a trust relationship between people, in that you keep it transparent and in regular view:

- **Make sure it's up-to-date** – First things first make sure the document is as accurate as you can get it before you try and start building people's trust in it.
- **Invite people to the document regularly** – Add it to your weekly reports, bookmark the links in your channels, and link people to it often. If a document is important, keep it as a living part of development, and ensure that it can be seen.
- **Have one source of truth, and link everything to it** – Often it's better to directly link to/include content from the central source of truth, such as the project milestones, than to duplicate it. It's easier to keep in-sync this way.
- **Keep it accountable** – Sharing the conclusions regularly and broadly allows people to step in and correct you/it. If you share the info every week, then it's never more than five working days out-of-date.

- **Cull documents that no one reads** – If you don't think anyone's reading it, stop writing it and see if anyone complains. It might not actually be helping your development, and this is the quickest way to find out.

MOTIVATING YOUR TEAM

Managers around the world are forever challenged with keeping their teams motivated.

There is an excellent talk given by Dan Pink for the Royal Society of Arts in which he lays out the factors that have been empirically observed to improve motivation[1]:

- **Security** – If people do not feel secure, then all their attention will be focused on making themselves safe. This security includes psychological safety, financial stability and security of their role. As referenced earlier, safer people take more creative risks and explore their talents more.
- **Autonomy** – Micromanaging is a common threat to autonomy; a manager constantly steps in, and comments on your method insisting it's done their way. In an autonomous environment, someone is given a goal, is trusted to reach it in their own way, then given feedback afterward. This allows them to go at their full pace and develop their ideas.
- **Mastery** – People want to get good at what they do. Artists want to improve, programmers want to learn, sound designers want to grow, and so on. If people feel like they are never going to have opportunities to improve in their craft, then their motivation will drop. I have changed jobs for this reason myself; I felt that my environment had no more opportunities for growth, and this would be better served with a contrasting environment.

To provide the motivation above, here are some methods you can employ:

- **Create a safe environment** – Ensure people are paid enough to survive, have the support networks they need, and create room to fail. This will attend to the security people need in order to accelerate and innovate.
- **Let them own their work** – When tasking out work, collaborate with the team so it's configured to their way and pace of working, then give them the space to take ownership. Highlight problems

if you see them, but ensure they are allowed to drive their solutions. Avoid telling them how to do things (unless they ask), as this detracts from their autonomy.

- **Have a clear mission** – Ensure the ultimate purpose of the project is clear, as are the goals of the feature. This helps with both security and autonomy, as people can feel safe in diving deep into their work and fully applying themselves to it, making their own decisions and adjustments with the shared goal in mind.
- **Use their strengths** – People want to show their skills, so lean into them. If they're good at brainstorming ideas, give them the experimental features. If they're good at planning and complex systems, then give them ownership of the features with the most depth. If they're good at leadership and communication, then give them a team to manage.
- **Give them challenges** – Look for opportunities to assign work that is more demanding/complicated than what they have handled so far, and give them clear, tangible chances to improve and grow. Make sure they've got support channels, so they don't just feel thrown in the deep end and abandoned.
- **Ensure they feel supported** – Whenever they have a problem you ideally want to be able to say "Don't worry, I'll deal with this. You're safe to carry on." If it's a problem they're heavily caught up in, then make it clear that you're going to help them through it, and that other support can be brought in as needed. This will help with their feeling of security.

JOANNA SKORUPA, SENIOR PRODUCER AT SUMO DIGITAL LTD

When Tim joined my team he came highly recommended. I was told that he was practically ready to be promoted to the next level, but to my surprise I watched Tim fail to impress over the coming months. His performance was inconsistent; it was clear he was capable, yet his efficiency wasn't there despite the relatively low workload compared to his peers. Once I realized that his attitude was also in slow decline, it became clear to me that there was more to it than just his skills level. Motivation fluctuates naturally, so it's important to take time to observe the individual in case the situation can resolve itself, however in this case, after a few months of getting to know Tim and providing him with my support, I knew a more substantial action was required.

When faced with an underperformer it's critical to understand the root cause of the issue, and oftentimes we may find that the individual is demotivated due to their needs not being met. As leaders it is our duty to support our teams and sometimes it may mean figuring out why someone's mood, attitude or efficiency is not meeting expectations. Removing outside factors, one's performance is not only dependent on the person's capability or work ethic; the games industry in particular is full of passionate people who want to do their job well and are driven by self-fulfillment. Purpose, the first element of the motivation magic formula, is not the problem for us, in most cases it's the reason why we joined the industry. Getting the difficulty balance right is just as important for the games we work on, as it is for our work-life. The right combination of easy and hard, as well as balancing the tasks the individual dislikes with ones they really enjoy is critical. Mastery is also very dependent on giving the right people the right opportunities, sensing when one is ready to advance on their journey, but also protecting people from being pushed into deep waters too early. Sense of control is a powerful motivator; traditional "old school" management may be leading to employee compliance; however, if we want engagement from our teams we should be striving for self-direction, that's why autonomy is in everyone's best interest.

Perhaps counter-intuitively to popular belief, the solution to Tim's demotivation was to trust him with more challenging work that suited his skills level more appropriately. Once he felt challenged, his level of engagement increased dramatically, as he finally felt valued. The transformation was so quick it left little space for people to doubt whether it was the right decision and Tim quickly became a pillar of the team's success.

LISTENING: THE QUIET SUPERPOWER

Listening is one of the most important tools in your toolbox. I'll explain why:

Listening helps you learn

It may seem obvious, but even with all the documentation in the world most of our learning comes from conversations with other people, when you hear their experience, ideas, and advice. If you want to grow as a producer, give everyone around you the space to talk, and you get to learn from each one of their unique perspectives.

Listening helps you understand other people

It can be all too easy to believe that people will act as we do, reason as we do, and feel as we do. However, people vary wildly from ourselves, and listening to what they have to say will illustrate this in the most surprising ways. Asking someone else's feelings about a situation will almost never quite match your own. Asking someone's approach to a situation will show evidence of completely different experiences and priorities to yours. As an expert communicator and builder of teams, a producer should take every opportunity to understand the people around them, and use this knowledge to help them all work together better.

Listening helps you build trust

We have all had the feeling that no one is listening to us, and it can be the most frustrating, enraging emotion that plagues our day-to-day lives. In the busy world of work where many people are stressed and fighting for their opinions to be heard it can seem harder than ever to have our own space to be listened to, even though we can solve the problem at hand or, even worse, we need help. If you can take the time to listen to people, and keep listening until they have said everything they needed to say, you can create that rare space in a busy world where that person got to feel seen, heard, and understood, and people will remember this.

Listening helps people feel validated

Many of your team members may arrive lacking confidence, or start to second-guess their own ideas after a setback. If you spend time giving air to their ideas, then they will feel that you respect them, their experience, and their opinions. If they voice an idea they are unsure about, and you validate it, then you help them resolve a small point of insecurity. This is also helpful when people are emotional or stressed; people in an emotional state usually aren't looking for someone to solve their problem, they are looking for someone to listen and give them a safe space for a moment while they wrangle with their own feelings.

Listening helps other people think

There is a semi-serious concept called "rubber duck debugging" which involves a programmer keeping a rubber duck on their desk and, whenever their code is not acting as expected, explaining the problems to it verbally.[2] If they stumble over their words, they know they have found where something is going wrong. You can be the "rubber duck" for your team members when they have a problem, listening while they talk through the issue, maybe asking some prompting questions (e.g., "How would this usually work?" "What have you tried so far?" "Have you had to solve this before?"), helping them step manually through their thoughts and find their solutions. This technique has enabled me to help the experts on my team overcome problems I don't actually understand.

"Active listening"

I first encountered the concept of "active listening" in a Jesse Schell GDC video called *Game Studio Leadership: You Can Do It* and it's been a great framework for tackling my own capabilities in listening, and I recommend it to all producers. There is plenty of literature out there, but here is the short version:

- **Understand your listening goal** – You may be listening to learn, to help with a problem, to understand a different perspective, or simply to give space to vent. Try to consciously identify your listening intention.
- **Give them your full attention** – Put away your phone and any other distractions, clearly face them, and show you're committing to listening.
- **Observe the whole person** – Pay attention to their tone of voice, choices of words, body language, and anything else that is going into their communicating.
- **Ask open, nonjudgmental questions** – Questions can show them that you're listening, and invite them to keep talking. Ensure the questions are nonaggressive and nonjudgmental so they don't feel the need to get defensive. You want them safe in your space.
- **Listen with an open mind** – Put off your own opinions for now, as they likely won't help you achieve your listening goal.
- **Resist the urge to interrupt** – You're giving them space, so put your own points aside for now. If you *do* find yourself interrupting, apologize and hand the conversation back to them.

- **Oh...and turn your camera on** – Listening is about making a connection with each other, so give the other person someone to connect to. I always turn my camera on if someone is talking to me, if just to clearly show I'm clearly listening.

PRESENTING: THE LOUD SUPERPOWER

There could be any number of reasons that you need to give a presentation. It could be a team status update, a walk-through of the results of a postmortem, or the pitching of a new game entirely. Suffice it to say that most producers will need to present information or ideas to other people, so it is valuable to invest in the skill of presenting.

My career has been full of presentations; I have lectured at universities on game audio, spoken at game jams on team-building, and toured one of the game industry's first talks on color-blindness to Develop:Brighton, GAConfEU in Paris, and GDC in San Francisco. Here is the process that I now follow when preparing a presentation (and most of this book, too!):

Identify the goal of your presentation

Much like all the work I have discussed in this book, having a clear goal will help you include the right ideas, support it with the right content, and finish it with the right ideas. Some example goals from past presentations of mine:

- "Inform the audience on an upcoming change to a development process well enough to provoke questions and get them prepared for the roll-out."
- "Advise our stakeholders on the nature of our budget predicament, explaining the events that led up to it, and providing detailed options to enable an informed decision."
- "Educate the audience about color blindness, the problems it creates for gamers, and furnish them with methods for improving the color-blind experience of their own games."

If you can understand the goal of your presentation, you can ensure each slide and point meets that goal, and keeps your presentation engaging and focused.

Identify your audience

I have given presentations to game industry veterans, business clients, CEOs, teammates, undergrads, college students and, in one case, a class of 5-year-old schoolchildren. Each time it has been essential to consider the nature of the audience, their existing knowledge, and their reason for listening. Bosses and clients will be purely interested in solutions and actions, conference attendees are looking for new ideas and entertainment, while university students mostly want to know how they get a job afterward. The nature of your audience should be closely related to the goal of your presentation and will be your main constraints for how that goal is achieved.

Introduce, explain, summarize

Every idea should have an adequate, high-level introduction, followed by an in-depth explanation, and a simple summary of the ideas expressed.

A good introduction can help prime the audience's understanding of what they are about to learn (e.g., "How to present well"), meaning they are both ready and invested to follow you through the details of the explanation. Afterward, you will want to repeat the key conclusions, frame the explanation practically, and provide an answer to your introduction (e.g., "To present well, do A, B, and C!").

One developer once shared with me a nice-and-concise version of this idea:

1. Tell them what you're going to tell them.
2. Tell them.
3. Tell them what you've told them.

I have found the "introduce, explain, summarize" method to be a simple and effective structure for a shared idea, and recommend applying it to both your presentation as a whole, and to every idea contained within it.

Design a learning journey for the listener

This is yet another place where a design-trained-mind can help a producer excel. Whenever I am putting together a presentation I try to understand the different components of the idea and how they relate to each other, allowing me to explain them separately and in the right order so that the listener is able to follow along and build the desired knowledge model.

For example, when building my color-blindness talk I identified the following components and sequence necessary to take a listener from knowing nothing about color-blindness to being able to design games that accommodated it. Here is the resulting sequence:

1. What the disability is.
2. Who it affects.
3. How it affects them.
4. How it affects me, the speaker.
5. How it affects playing video games.
6. Why developing for it is hard.
7. Offer solutions for this problem.
8. Give real examples of these solutions.
9. Summarize with the solutions as the takeaways.

Each learning journey will be different, but taking the time to map this out when planning the presentation will help ensure your audience can absorb what you are trying to teach.

End with clear, actionable takeaways

In many cases, a presentation is intended to inspire some kind of action from the audience member, so you want to be utterly clear what that action is. This should be done through a final summary of actionable takeaways at the end. These should first be surfaced individually as you go through each point in the presentation, and then summarized as a sort of "to-do list" at the end.

There's a big difference between a "factual" takeaway and an "actionable" takeaway, for example:

• Factual takeaway – Cars are dangerous.
• *Actionable* takeaway – Look both ways when crossing roads.

If you are calling for action, ensure your takeaways are clear on this. Otherwise, while your audience may have found the talk interesting, they might not be clear on what they're supposed to do with this new knowledge.

Rehearse

In the same way that "rubber duck debugging" can help a programmer find problems in their code, rehearsing presentations can help you find your problems ahead of the actual performance. At the bare minimum do a rehearsal on your own, standing up, facing an empty room, and speaking aloud. You can feel how your voice projects, how you stand, and as you speak you can find where your words falter, which can clue you in to the bits that you need to think about more.

If possible, do a rehearsal with one or two peers, who will then be able to tell you anything that didn't make sense, which will help you improve the quality of the presentation, and ensure that your ideas come across properly.

Slides should be visual aids, not text

The most common mistake with presentation slides is to dump all the information on them in huge paragraphs that go past too fast to read. People don't need more words on the screen, when they're already listening to you. Any slides should reinforce the idea you're expressing, whether an image, a data graphic, a stock photo, or even a meme! If the point you're making is emotional, then back it up with an emotional image. If factual, then show a factual example. In truth, some of the best presentations I've seen have basically been a rant where the slides were completely irrelevant. Consider the stand-up comedian who, with a suitably designed journey, can carry an audience with no slides at all through a wide range of ideas.

Presentation skills are a great asset to a producer; they enable you to educate teams, create positive change, build your professional profile, and are essential for pitching new features, games, and strategies to "the people with the money." For these reasons, a producer that can present well will be trusted by peers and leaders alike and vastly empowered in their career.

TEACHING

You can't use SCRUM if no one knows what it is. A lot of producer work involves aligning team processes and tools, and cross-educating developers about each other's methods, technologies, processes, and working language.

Even more so when you start *inventing* processes and have to explain them to everyone else.

To prepare for this, it's worth investing in your ability to teach your team. Here are some options to consider when teaching something new:

Face-to-face teaching

Often the simplest method to teach someone is just to talk them through the idea or method in person. For this there are a few tips to keep it successful:

- **Demonstrate, then invite** – When showing a method, first demonstrate it to show the clear outcome, then hand it over
- **Use their screen instead of yours** – People learn far more effectively when they are the one taking action. Get them to share their screen, and direct them to complete each step, so they can build the "muscle memory," and remain fully engaged throughout.
- **Be patient** – The way we explain things doesn't always match the way people expect explanations, and sometimes we clash. The idea might not click until *just* the right question is answered in *just* the right way, so be patient with each other.

Written guides

One of the most obvious methods of teaching in a software environment is writing a guide or document.

- **Keep sentences short** – A list of instructions is much easier to read than a huge prosaic paragraph.
- **Use headings** – Most writing software have headings format presets to help you give your documents a good look, and break them up in a visually pleasing way.
- **Use screenshots/Gifs** – In the digital age, there are so many tools for quickly gathering still and moving images to paste into your documents, and they will make your guides far more effective.
- **Get someone to check it** – Ask a colleague to review your document and provide feedback before rolling it out to a whole team.

Video tutorials

If you find you are explaining something long and complicated again and again, consider recording a video. You don't need advanced video-editing tools, just record a solo conference call with yourself while sharing your screen. An even better option is to record the call in which you are teaching another person, as this will also contain their questions and your answers, providing further information.

Presentations

As discussed earlier, presentations are a good accompaniment when rolling out a new idea or sharing the basics of an idea to a large group very quickly. They can also carry the advantage of being followed by Q&A sessions, which can quickly get all of the initial questions answered right at the start while the whole group is present.

Practice exercises (in groups where possible)

This might feel like going back to school, but the quickest way to ensure someone has learned something is to do it. If, for example, you are teaching a team a new 3D model export pipeline, then it can be a good idea to get the team on a call, and have them try exporting a model at the same time. You can talk them all through the process, answer questions, and troubleshoot as you go, and by the end of it everyone will have at least one bout of experience in the new skill.

All the above methods are effective and should be used in combination. One of my best ways of learning, which then plays into my teaching, is writing my documentation *while* I learn something new. This builds my knowledge quickly, and immediately enables me to explain the method to someone else with a document ready.

CONSTRUCTIVE CRITICISM – GIVING FEEDBACK THAT EMPOWERS

Throughout your career there will be times when you need to provide some criticism. Maybe you are giving feedback on their creative work, telling them a process isn't working, or even asserting a need to change their behavior. It is very easy for criticism to come across as harsh, dismissive, and downright insulting, and the other person can often get defensive in these situations.

While you cannot control the behavior of others, there are some techniques you can apply to shape your criticism into something helpful, constructive, and even welcome:

Feedback should be a critique of a specific work or behavior, not of a person's character

It's very easy to use the phrase "you are very X" when giving feedback, which can put a person on the defensive as they weren't interested in a commentary on the nature of their personality, they just wanted to know if they were doing a good job! A more collaborative way of criticizing can be referring to the actions being taken. For example if a teammate's pushy conversation style is causing problems, instead of saying to them "you're too pushy" you could say that "when you push too hard in conversation, it can shut people down." This allows the other person to separate the problem from themselves, and work on it with less threat of taking offense.

Marshall B. Rosenberg's book *Nonviolent Communication: A Language of Life* goes into these kinds of conversation mechanics in great detail and can provide some good tools for reflecting on our natural communication style.

Feedback should be goal-driven

Whenever giving feedback, it should be in aim of approaching a clear goal, which will help give clarity to the other person, and help them improve their decision-making. For example, you can say that a character's design is too flashy, but this isn't helpful unless you can point out the goal being missed; perhaps the game is intended to be grounded and familiar and the design should go more in that direction.

Feedback should educate with context

People will do the best job they can with the information they have, but that information is often not complete. When making *Halo Wars 2* we found that the initial sounds created for the marines' assault rifle were unusable; each shot had five or more different components, which made sense for a first-person shooter where only a couple of guns would be fired in any moment, but it wouldn't work in our strategy game with hundreds of assault rifles firing at the same time and viewed from a sky-high perspective. This is where providing the additional context in our feedback could enable the correct artistic and technical decisions to be made.

Feedback should highlight the problems, but not necessarily prescribe the solution

Particularly when dealing with creative work, it can be tempting to say "Oh just do this," lean in, and do it for them. A key example is the taboo of giving a "line read" when recording an actor speaking dialogue; this is what they call it if you say "just say it like this" and do the line yourself. This is micro-management and feels patronizing without helping the performer improve the application of their craft. Instead, you should give the feedback, then invite the other person to suggest solutions. You can give opinions, but drawing it from their understanding will help them be autonomous and effective in that creative space.

Feedback should be kind

Everyone working on your game is your collaborator, and you should take some responsibility for making sure at least one part of their working environment is pleasant, that part being you. Aggressive, demeaning feedback may make you feel powerful in the moment, but it will not help your team members feel safe, improve skills, or make better games. Be kind with your criticism, and remember that you want all your collaborators to succeed, so you should empower them all where you can.

To summarize the above paragraphs, here are some direct steps to making sure that your feedback is constructive and empowering:

1. Criticize the work, not the person
2. Refer to the goal
3. Educate on the context
4. Highlight the problem, but let them solve it
5. Be kind with your comments

HOW TO WRITE AN EMAIL THAT PEOPLE ACTUALLY READ

Emails can be a very useful tool, but can also be a complete waste of time and words when done wrong. We're all used to receiving emails that are huge walls of text, and after 5 minutes of reading we conclude that there is no action for us.

Emails can, however, be an extremely powerful communication tool, so let's look at how to get it right:

Why use email at all?

With our instant messages and documentation wikis now, you could argue that email is outdated and no longer helpful, but I argue it serves a separate purpose to this. In my opinion, an email is a good idea when the following is required:

- **Searchability** – Emails are generally easier to search and archive than instant messages, so if your sent information will need to be referenced later on (e.g., dates, major decisions, new practices, etc.), then an email is a good idea.
- **Accountability** – If you are communicating in a process where decisions need to be in-writing and accountable, then email is the best option as it provides a searchable paper trail for decisions and communications.
- **Large audience** – A broadcasted email is an easy way to ensure large groups of people are exposed to a message, and if your aim is to be transparent on a difficult issue, then email is a better option than messaging.
- **Importance** – If the topic is extremely important, then it should be communicated in as many channels as possible, including email. One advantage of email is that it is less likely to get lost than a message in a busy channel, as generally people receive fewer emails than messages.

How to ruin an email

The main problem one can have with an email is not knowing what it wants. Much like with your reports, the first question on every reader's mind is "Do

I have to do anything?", and if it takes them several paragraphs to find out the answer is "no," then their time has been wasted. Worse still, they may decide they're too busy to read all that text and miss out on the call to action entirely.

There are a couple of ways this problem is caused:

- **Too much prose** – Paragraph after paragraph can be very draining to read, when short bullet points would have carried the same action in a much more digestible way.
- **Important information is buried** – Connected to the first problem, if the important, action driving information requires the user to scroll down and spot it among the text and images, it can easily be missed or deemed unimportant.
- **No "call to action"** – You can fill an email with facts and data, but if the reader's required actions are not clearly stated, then the reader may not even realize something is being asked of them, or that they should take any action at all.

Writing an email the right way

In order to avoid these issues, and increase the chances that your email will successfully communicate, here are some tips:

- **Include the "call to action" in the subject line** – If the email is a request for a sign-off, write "SIGN-OFF REQUEST," or if it is an update to a process write "PROCESS UPDATE." Make it as obvious as possible what the email is for.
- **Put the "call to action" clearly at the top** – Answer the question of "Do I need to do anything?" before writing anything else. I will often start an email with "Hello person X, we want to know which of the following options you prefer for handling topic Y," and then give the details below. The same applies for mass emails, for example, if you will need all users to restart their machines that day, then start the email with "We require you to restart your machine by 23:59 pm tonight," and then go on to explain why.
- **Put key points in headings** – It's ok to have large emails, as long as you make them easy to navigate. Break up the email by sections and put clear headings in each section. Sometimes you can even link anchors to a "Contents" section at the top, so people can click directly to the bit they care about.

- **Details in bullet points** – To reduce prose, use bullet points wherever possible. They are a much more digestible way to present multiple points in written text.
- **Accompany all data with a summary** – If you are showing data, ensure there is a written summary explaining in writing the important conclusion. Don't give the reader the work of parsing the data to understand what you're trying to say.

If you want to go deeper into the art of "good email writing," then I recommend looking to the world of marketing; there are tons of articles online for "how to write a good marketing email" and these are the best in the business, as their email-writing skill directly relate to the growth and success of their business. I can also recommend the book *Don't Make Me Think* by Steve Krug which shares a lot of excellent advice on information perception that you can apply to your own communication work.

ANTICIPATING QUESTIONS

In *The Expanse* novel series by James S. A. Corey, one character repeatedly uses the phrase "Once is never. Twice is always" to describe the actions of other people. This is a rule I also apply to the questions I get asked at work; if someone asks the same question twice, assume they're *always* going to ask that question. Good producers will understand this and will work to anticipate these questions when preparing for meetings, presenting information, and designing reports. It is the mark of a mature, organized producer, and here are my tips for achieving this for yourself:

Keep an "FAQ" of the questions that you regularly get asked

I keep a list on the side while I work, and any time someone asks me a question I add it to the list. Here are the usual suspects:

- When will feature X be delivered?
- Who is working on feature X?
- What is the team doing this week?
- *How* is the team doing this week?
- Are we on track for milestone Y?

There are obviously many more, but the key is to understand what you're being asked. This can inform the information you will need to regularly provide.

Build methods to obtain this information regularly

Now that you know what information you are being asked for, you can start setting yourself up to always know what you need to know. Here are some example methods I use to do this:

- Subscribe to task-tracking filters that answer the question for me.
- Create data dashboards that answer the question for me.
- Set up regular meetings with these questions on the agenda.
- Design a regular report based on these questions, thus giving me a routine of finding the answers, writing them down, and sharing them.

If, through all these methods, you can create an environment where people always have the answers to their questions before they even need to ask, you will be accelerating your team, and building for yourself a reputation for always being on top of your work.

OPINIONS VS EXPECTATIONS – EFFECTIVE NEGOTIATION

I had an experience at FundamentalVR which completely changed the way I negotiate when making decisions and compromises with other people.

For a while I was having a conflict with a peer; he was insisting that we had to complete all the features promised to our client at all cost, and I was arguing that it couldn't be done with the time and resources remaining. We were at an impasse with him saying "We've got to" and me saying "We can't" and we were getting nowhere. Then at one point in the conversation I tried something different, and instead of saying "We can't," I instead chose to say "Ok, here is what I expect to happen…" and laid out my predicted, data-driven timeline of events and deliveries and, to my surprise, his behavior changed immediately! He looked at everything, thought about it, and then went away to come up with some new options based on what I'd shown him.

It shocked me how abruptly this went from impasse to action, so I have endeavored to shape all of my negotiating conversations around this method of using expectations rather than opinions. Here's my understanding:

Opinions are subjective, expectations are objective

When someone is sharing an opinion on something it can often be hard to relate to it because it is from their subjective perspective. When I was sharing my opinion of "We can't do this work," it contained a lot of unspoken assumptions and values, such as not wanting the team to crunch, and not wanting to demand yet more resources from our central teams.

In contrast, the expectation I shared was based on empirical data, which could be objectively verified. Even if no one has the time to verify the data, even knowing that the expectation was data-driven builds confidence that it is a more reliable conviction than my subjective opinion.

Opinions are value-based, expectations are impact-based

One time at Creative Assembly I was arguing for reprioritization of a subtitle system for a public demo, at first insisting simply that "we needed it." It wasn't working; I had shared a value, but it wasn't a match for the team's priorities. Subtitles were scheduled for much later in the project and weren't important up-front. It wasn't until I was able to articulate the impact, where players in text-only localizations wouldn't be able to understand the instructions that the team agreed that something needed to be done. Impacts are much easier for others to consider than values.

Opinions are obstructive, expectations are empowering

I think the main impact of this change is that opinions can often seem obstructive and can feel like a bit of a power struggle of whose opinion is more important. When sharing an expectation the opposite is true; an expectation shared is empowering for all parties involved, as it provides information that enables further decision-making. People are always far more ready to act when they are empowered by what you say, and education is a key form of empowerment.

I find the above an extremely helpful concept in my day-to-day communication. Of course, you can still express opinions in your day-to-day work, but if you are in a situation where a group of you are struggling to reach consensus on a decision, then try switching to communication expectations to clarify the way forward.

THE POWER OF THE STUPID QUESTION

Whenever I hear the phrase "there are no stupid questions" I see it as a challenge.

Joking aside, being able to ask what seems like the most basic question is an extremely powerful tool in sharing knowledge across a team. I am often in meetings with people of such extraordinary expertise in fields I can barely fathom; artists talking about Fresnel equations, audio teams discussing azimuth angles, and programmers talking about…well, anything. As such, I often need to betray this ignorance by asking what they're talking about. Showing a lack of knowledge in this way can be frightening for some people, but I have learned to relish it. I fill my knowledge gaps faster, I earn trust through the display of humility and, most importantly, I get the question answered for all the people in the room who also needed to know *but were too scared to ask*. I have long lost count of how many times I have received a message during a meeting reading "Thank you for asking that. I didn't know either!"

This doesn't just apply to expert knowledge; every company comes with its own language, history, and cultural elements that long-term employees just assume everyone knows, so again it's worth asking the questions. "Who is Bobby?" "What's an 'uplift'?" "Why is everyone upset about the number 5.9?" I remember a meeting at Creative Assembly where we were planning a large-scale team presentation, and we discussed how the nearby theater would not be viable as a venue "because it was panto season." After a couple of mentions of this our American Director of Production raised his hand and said "Speaking as a foreigner…what's 'panto season'?" We then explained how "panto" refers to the pantomime stage productions that occupy all major theaters in the UK during the Christmas period. A useful lesson for the mostly British team

Never be afraid to ask the Stupid Question. It empowers you and the people around you with both knowledge and confidence.

REFERENCES

1. Dan Pink, RSA ANIMATE: Drive: The surprising truth about what motivates us [Internet]. Youtube; [cited 2024 Oct 17]. Available from: https://www.youtube.com/watch?v=u6XAPnuFjJc&ab_channel=RSA
2. RubberDuckDebugging.Rubberduckdebugging[Internet].Rubberduckdebugging.com. [cited 2024 Oct 17]. Available from: https://rubberduckdebugging.com/

One more team member *You* 10

Of all the people you will be managing in your game career, your biggest responsibility will be yourself. You will be responsible for not just your work, but also your attitude, your decisions, and your health. This chapter is all about how you can invest in yourself as a professional, grow yourself to be ready for challenges, and protect your energy and motivation on your own terms.

GROWING AND LEARNING

When I started as a producer I knew almost nothing about the job. I'd heard of sprints, and I had some experience managing audio QA testers, but all my capabilities as a producer have come from years of learning; developing new skills, acquiring new knowledge, and working on my attitude. The more I grow, the more I enjoy the job, and can find fulfillment in more and more challenging roles.

There are a lot of ways to acquire knowledge, and you will find different ones that appeal to you, depending on your lift routine and how you learn best, but here is a quick coverage of what you can look into.

Books

Obviously, books are an excellent way to learn. There are not that many books on game production itself, but there is endless writing on the myriad of skills that go into production. There are books on project management, team motivation, game design, work psychology, information design, public

DOI: 10.1201/9781003519065-10

speaking, business studies, difficult conversations, self-confidence, and so on. All of these can help to grow your skill set as an organizer of talented people.

Producers can also benefit from the stories of other developers. There are many books sharing the roller-coaster rides of developing games out there (the most reputed being *Blood Sweat & Pixels* by Jason Schrier), and these can provide a grounding perspective on how endlessly challenging game development is.

Here are three of my favorite books for having helped me develop as a producer:

- *Turn the Ship Around!* by L, David Marquet – Lessons in building teams of autonomous leaders from a US Navy submarine commander.
- *The Culture Map* by Erin Meyer – Observations in the subtle differences in business culture around the world. Great for opening your mind to different.
- *The Design of Everyday Things* by Don Norman – One of the best books for understanding how people perceive their interactions with the world, which is great for helping to design effective and intuitive processes.

Videos

In the age of YouTube, there is a tutorial on *everything*. Any time you start working with a new tool, or start working in a new methodology, watch some onboarding videos to quickly broaden your applicable knowledge. If you can get a license, the GDC vault is an astonishing archive of all the talks from the Game Developer Conference throughout the years. TED talks are also great for new ideas on team leadership, work psychology, and self-care. It's such an amazing time to be alive to have instant access to so much informative video content and worth taking full advantage of.

Group training

Wherever possible sign up for group training sessions, especially if work is paying for them. Group sessions can be the best way to improve your interpersonal skills such as presenting, active listening, and conflict resolution. The people around you will also contribute their own perspectives and thoughts to the sessions, so you can be learning from each other, and if they are your colleagues you can carry on this journey together right back into your job.

Online courses

The internet is increasingly full of digital courses you can take to learn about almost anything. My most valuable undertaking was a Udemy course on Excel VBA (Visual Basic for Applications) which taught me to start programming my own macros into spreadsheets and enabled me to start building more advanced production tools for myself and my teams. Some example platforms are LinkedIn Learning for leadership and management, Skillshare for creativity and design, and Udemy for pretty much *everything*.

Conferences and networking

I love conferences; even when I'm not sitting in on talks from some of the greatest teachers in the game industry I'm surrounded by developers who all just want to talk about game development, which is beyond energizing for me. Every conference I learn just as much – if not more – from the random spiraling conversations I have with other developers, sharing their niche experiences with a transparency found in few other industries. Game conferences can be a super-charger for your knowledge and drive, and I can't recommend them enough.

I have been a game development professional for 14 years at time of writing, learning every day, and I expect to learn even more for the rest of my career. It is a welcome journey that never ends, so look out for these learning opportunities:

- Read the books
- Watch the videos
- Take the courses
- Train with your peers
- Talk to everyone about everything

Last thing on learning; in my opinion it almost doesn't matter which books you read, which videos you watch, and which courses you take, just *keep learning something* and you will invest in yourself for the rest of your life.

RECEIVING FEEDBACK

One of the best pieces of feedback I was ever given was when my lead producer told me that, when asked to do something, I would say "No" and argue that it wouldn't work. This would create a situation where he had come to me for assistance, and wouldn't get it. He wanted me to understand that he was really asking for help with achieving a goal, and even if his suggestion wasn't ideal that I should work with him to find a solution, rather than just saying "No." I was quite stubborn in my early career, and it took a while for me to internalize this advice, but as I look back it was genuinely good, constructive feedback, intended to empower me to be a more helpful collaborator. Reflecting on this, I would suggest the following thoughts when receiving feedback:

They're not your enemy

It's very rare in the world of work that someone is actually out to get you, and most people are really just trying to get on with their life and make good games. Remember this, and trust that their feedback is not meant to bring you down, but help you align with them on the goal of the team.

Be humble

Everyone makes mistakes, and no one knows everything. If you can internalize the fact that you will always be an imperfect person doing an imperfect job, it can be much easier to take feedback without it feeling like an insult to your abilities or character. Accept that tomorrow you will be better than today you, and sometimes feedback is what can make the difference.

Ask for feedback regularly

If what you want is to grow throughout your career, then remember that every piece of feedback, advice, and criticism is an opportunity for this growth. Ask for feedback regularly; get people to check your emails, ask peers if they understand your processes, and invite criticism on the way you run meetings. This will also build a degree of trust in your team, as it shows you value their opinion, and feel safe enough with them to let them be honest with you.

Good advice can be badly given

You won't always be surrounded by good communicators, and there will be times that "feedback" comes in the form of an abrupt outburst, a passive-aggressive comment, or a moaning whinge. While it is tempting to ignore everything said in rudeness, you're only sabotaging yourself by doing so. If you can, take a breath and say "Keep going, I'm listening" which opens the door to find the constructive elements of their opinion, giving you a chance to get good advice from bad communicators.

Of course, I will also encourage you to give feedback on *their* communication style, as well. It's a better environment if everyone can communicate well.

Listen to all advice (but you don't always have to act on it)

Everyone has a different perspective, journey and set of priorities, and a lot of advice will be earnest and well-meaning, but may not be right for your situation. Take the time to listen to everyone's advice, as it can only give you *more* opportunities for growth, not fewer.

DAVID BOWMAN – CHIEF OPERATING OFFICER AT XR GAMES

It can be frustrating seeing so many people give up time and effort to create something great and expressive, and then have some distant stakeholder say "More blue." It's extremely common to get trite, unhelpful, and unkind feedback. It can have an emotional impact, and it's worth preparing for this, and figuring out how you can stay positive, and be satisfied with your own contribution. You and your team are creating art, which is always emotional, and never done. If you have given of yourself, without destroying yourself, then you have done the right thing. If you have been there and helped your team to create a new expression out of nothing, and created a new experience that touches people emotionally, then you don't need to let "More blue" get to you.

"I INTEND TO..." AND "DELIBERATE ACTION" – TWO TECHNIQUES FOR TAKING ACTION WITH CONFIDENCE

As mentioned earlier, one of my favorite books on leadership is David L Marquet's *Turn the Ship Around!,* which tells of Marquet's journey to overhaul a dysfunctional, hierarchical submarine crew into an empowered, collaborative unit. While the whole book is full of great advice for team empowerment, there are two of Marquet's mechanisms that I employ every day in my job. These techniques help me stay proactive and help ensure my actions are on the right course.

"I intend to…"

In short, the phrase "I intend to" is a phrase that Marquet's crew started to use when communicating to him, taking the place of "Requesting permission to…." Their goal was to free the crew from being constrained by waiting for a single person to give the orders for everything that happened. The result was that his team on the sub would decide upon their own actions and then declare them to him with enough context to approve the action in confidence, ideally without having to ask any prior questions. In my role I use this all the time. Rather than wait for my superiors to have all the good ideas, or wait for their input before I decide to do anything, I will look at my situation, decide on my best course of action, and message it to any relevant stakeholders. Then I would just get on with it at my own pace.

"Take deliberate action"

After one too many small – but potentially dangerous – errors in their training exercises, Marquet and his team decided they didn't want their team to make mistakes anymore. They identified the problem as people acting without thinking, and so they started a practice of "deliberate action" which involves declaring aloud what you are about to do; this gives both yourself and the people around you the opportunity to interrupt the action if required. For this reason, when I arrived as a producer on the Total War audio team I would voice all my intentions for new processes aloud to my manager. There were indeed a few times where she stopped me; the process I wanted to change had been purposefully designed and the team were still quietly dependent on it. This prevented me from making several disruptive mistakes. I generally share my screen whenever I'm updating information during a call, as my colleagues can sometimes call out that I've mis-interpreted an idea, or that there's even a better way to do what I'm doing. It's extremely effective for improving the quality of the work I do.

The mechanisms of "I intend to…" and "Take Deliberate Action" combine to achieve a highly proactive and transparent method of working in which I am always taking action, never waiting for permission, and always receiving course corrections when required. I recommend these to all producers, as it can help you act faster and more effectively in service of your teams.

UNDERSTANDING YOUR BANDWIDTH

While you are likely measuring the workloads and protecting the bandwidth of the people around you, there's probably no-one doing the same for you, and producers can get VERY busy indeed.

We often are involved with multiple teams, with sprawling responsibilities, and every problem is our problem. Working on multiple projects can make this even worse, as each project can exert a whole producer's worth of pressure on its own, meaning you are now pulled in multiple directions with everyone saying their work is your top priority. The way to a healthy production role is not about finding an environment free from stress and pressure, but by building methods that let you endure these environments without burning out. Here are some methods I use to stay sane in crazy times:

Accept that your work will never run out

Production isn't like content creation in that there is no distinct list of tasks for you to finish and go home. Instead, producers are always scanning for problems, hunting for process optimizations, and seeking opportunities to evolve the team. By definition this is work that will never run out, and so you will have to get used to the idea that you will be leaving work – every day – with unfinished business in the office. You can carry it on tomorrow.

Decide on a minimum acceptable output for yourself

I have observed a few activities that I consider essential, regular parts of my job that then go on to enable the other less consistent activities, and have come to regard this as a bar for being able to tell when I'm getting too busy:

- I clear my Slack every morning
- I get through my emails every day
- I don't skip any meetings
- I do my reports each week

If any of these criteria are not being met, then something is wrong, and I'm probably going to start dropping the ball soon, as I don't have enough time to attend to all the required communication. These criteria can be scaled to if you are handling multiple projects at once, as it can demonstrate an effective minimum support for each project.

I suggest you consider your own job, and make a decision on what your own minimum daily/weekly support should look like, and speak up if you're falling behind on that minimum.

Look ahead, and tell your manager when you think you're going to "drop the ball"

One time at FundamentalVR I did exactly this; I was on several projects that were all coming to release phases in the same month, and these are the most time-consuming, hands-on part of the project for the producer. I could see these all coming to a head in the same month, and I knew that it was going to be more than I could fully support, so I told the production managers that I was expecting to start missing things in that time. This enabled them to take some action to support me; they found another producer with some bandwidth to support me, freeing up some time, and they also shared some priorities, advised me on processes that could fail with less consequence, and that they would back me up in the case of any such failures.

Let poorly planned things fail

Early in my career a programmer shared with me the quote "Your poor planning does not constitute my emergency," which I stick by. The truth is that sometimes you will be set up with a situation which can never succeed, the most common being that too much work is being demanded for too soon a deadline. It can be easy to panic, dive into weeks of painful overtime, miss the deadline anyway, and blame yourself for the whole thing. Instead I advise you simply do your best, stay transparent, but go home on time, and if your superiors cannot engineer a success out of the situation they have handed to you, then this will have to be *their* lesson. They may also be more likely to discuss how to improve things than they would if you had burned yourself to a crisp to deliver, only for them to say "it worked last time" and do the same again.

As a summary, here are the techniques you can use to be an effective guardian of your own bandwidth:

- **Work never runs out, so go home on time**
- **Figure out your "minimum output"**
- **Look ahead and tell your managers about upcoming busy times**
- **Better the bad plan fails than you burn out**

PRACTICE EFFECTIVE
LAZINESS – AUTOMATE YOURSELF

I never send meeting agendas anymore. It's the same email every week, so rather than do that manually I will just set up a repeated mailbot – with an automatically updated date – that links to the agenda doc. It provides a consistent form of communication that doesn't rely on my memory or availability. I take every opportunity I can to automate my own work; it saves me time, reduces the errors in my work, and can keep processes going while I attend to the rest of my job. Here are some key automation opportunities:

Spreadsheet macros

Spreadsheets form such a large part of the producer's working day that it is one of the best bang-for-buck places to automate your work. Clever formulas can handle all your calculations for you, a recorded macro means you can replace a tedious manual process with a keyboard shortcut, and more detailed macros can be programmed to create whole tools.

Task manager automations

When I discovered that I could subscribe to filters in Jira, it was like hiring a whole new producer just for me. Using this tool I get several emails every day from Jira telling me exactly what I've programmed it for; errors in tickets, new work on my team, tasks that haven't been updated in 5 days, and more.

Messaging workflows

All the new messaging tools now have APIs for building automated processes; Slack has its workflow builder, Teams has Power Automate, and Discord can integrate endless apps to automate messages, forms, channel assignments, and more. Look at the options in your tools, and play around with them. A particular advantage of bringing automations into the message tools is that your whole company is there, so you can easily share the benefits of these workflows with everyone.

Artificial Intelligence

There is so much noise around AI at the moment, and it's hard to know exactly what's going to happen, but I fully expect that a lot of this technology will directly augment the work of producers. I'm expecting smart search engines for project documentation, language-model bots for booking meetings, and chat-bots to assist with data analysis. Microsoft's Copilot already takes better meeting notes than I do. I advise all producers to look closely into the coming technologies, play with them, and be the first to take advantage of any technology that can empower you.

To quote a line that Bill Gates probably never said (according to Factly[1]), "I will always choose a lazy person to do a hard job, because he will find an easy way to do it." Producers should embrace this laziness with an inventor's fervor and automate every single task that they can.

PROTECTING YOURSELF FROM BURNOUT

If your bandwidth gets out of control, then you can be at risk of burnout. WebMD defines burnout as "a form of exhaustion caused by constantly feeling swamped."[2] This can lead to feeling physically, mentally, and emotionally drained, both in and out of the job. It is often a vicious cycle as your work performance decreases, but then your workload starts piling up even more, and you are increasingly incapable of handling the exhaustion. This can have seriously damaging effects on your health and home life.

All too often we see game professionals going through burnout at some point in their career, and then the only course is a sustained break from the job to recover, sometimes never coming back. It is inarguably better to avoid this situation entirely, and to that end there are some techniques you can use to protect yourself from this burnout.

Take frequent breaks

When I was a game tester at Microsoft they mandated taking 15-minute breaks in both the morning and the afternoon, as well as the hour break for lunch. Taking breaks is essential for giving yourself a chance to breathe and relax and is key to a healthy work routine. If possible, move to a different environment like the office kitchen, or better yet, leave the office entirely and spend some time somewhere completely different to help your brain reset. Some people use a technique called "pomodoro" to help with a balance of focus and breaks; a single pomodoro is 25 minutes of work followed by a 5–10 minute break, and after four pomodoros you take a longer break or 30 minutes or more, with the timings often being managed by an alarm or app.[3]

Ask for help

If you are getting snowed under with work, then it's time to ask for help. You can rarely "work harder" your way out of a burnout situation, so ask for help with your responsibilities. Sometimes the situation can be resolved by shifting a deadline, or reducing the deliverables, but the best method is usually splitting the responsibilities onto someone else, especially with producer burnout. The demands are usually ad hoc and uncontrolled, so you'll need to reduce the amount of things you are accountable for.

If you are finding that you are lying awake at night still thinking about your spreadsheets, hardly sleeping, and coming to work the next day drained and despairing, then the burnout is already setting in and now the person you should be asking for help is your doctor. Tell them the situation and ask for a sick note.

Never sprint to the finish (because it's never the finish)

When approaching a major deadline the urgency of the studio tends to pick up, new decisions come in quicker and the pressure starts building on everyone. Despite this, you should resist extra demands and overtime as much as possible because although this may feel like a finish line, it never is. Even when your game releases, you will still need to be in the studio the next day, fully awake, and ready to deal with the hotfix issues. You should look to build a sustainable pace of work that you can continue through both the high pressure and low pressure times, as there will always be more important work next week.

Update your CV and get ready to leave

One of the things I often see contributing to some people's burnout is that they are trapped in the job; they can't imagine going anywhere else. This means that when their job becomes unhealthy they can't bargain for anything better. If your work environment is becoming a risk to your health, and there is no sign of improvement or relent, then update your CV and look for somewhere healthier.

They're just games, and it's just a job, but your health is your entire life. To recap, here are some techniques to use:

- **Take breaks from work to rest and recharge**
- **Ask for help whenever you need it**
- **Don't exceed your sustainable pace of work**
- **Leave if there is no sign of respite**

MEASURING YOUR OWN SUCCESS

It can often be hard to identify good production.

In a 2024 TEDx talk in Berlin, Martin Gutmann talked about the strange difference in how we perceive leaders.[4] He compares the two polar explorers Ernest Shackleton and Roald Amundsen; how Shackleton has become legend through books, films, and documentaries despite the fact that all his voyages were disasters, and how Amundsen has fallen largely into obscurity despite succeeding time and time again (he was first to both North and South Poles and to navigate the Northwest Passage). Gutmann claims that the reason we talk far more about leaders who failed is because they make so much more noise and create much more drama, leading us to believe they took more action. It is telling that the only Apollo space mission to be dramatized in cinema (twice, as of 2024) is the disastrous Apollo 13 where the astronauts were nearly lost. The most famous ship in history – The Titanic – sunk on its maiden voyage.

Annoyingly, this "action fallacy" (as Gutmann describes it) applies to production as well; when you are doing a good job there is curiously little to talk about. Deadlines are met, bugs are fixed, and developers are calm and healthy. This can make it very challenging to know if you are doing a good job, but I have developed a few techniques for myself to track this, which I suggest trying out for yourself:

Note your own successes

Delivering a feature on time is a success. Streamlining a process is a success. Teaching someone a new technique is a success. I suggest keeping a sort of diary for whenever you achieve something that feels noteworthy *to you*. This list isn't for communicating to other people – it's unlikely it will be very exciting to them – instead it is to give you something you can occasionally refer back to, and see a list growing of your positive impact on the team and project.

Celebrate the problems solved

Whenever there is a problem solved on the team, you can make a *lot* more noise about it. If something is clearly solved, send a message to the channel, and tell people about it; good news can be a morale builder for others as well. You can also record wins regularly in reports or team presentations which can add some readable substance to the progress you and your team are making.

Observe differences in retrospectives

There have been many times when I have joined a team, and in the first retrospective the major complaints have been about communication. Multiple times I have been able to observe that – as I work with the team to solve various problems – communication shifts from the list of "stuff going badly" to the list of "stuff going well." I generally take this as a sign that I am helping the situation (at least, I'm not making it worse!). If you have regular retrospectives you can do the same; observe the changes in the topics being reported over time. If the retrospectives are starting to get quiet, then it's likely you're doing a *really* good job!

To reflect on the above, it is really important to be able to get to a stage where you have a positive self-image as a professional, and this often needs evidence to support. In this strange environment where the output of good production is "normal boring life," remember the above techniques:

- **Keep a private list of small successes**
- **Make a public show of each problem you help solve**
- **Use retrospectives as a tool to measure your own performance**

REFERENCES

---

1. Mandadi A. There is no evidence to state that Bill Gates made this statement about choosing a lazy person to do a hard job [Internet]. FACTLY. 2022 [cited 2024 Oct 30]. Available from: https://factly.in/there-is-no-evidence-to-state-that-bill-gates-made-this-statement-about-choosing-a-lazy-person-to-do-a-hard-job/

2. Burnout: Symptoms and signs [Internet]. WebMD. [cited 2024 Oct 30]. Available from: https://www.webmd.com/mental-health/burnout-symptoms-signs

3. Wikipedia contributors. Pomodoro Technique [Internet]. Wikipedia, The Free Encyclopedia. 2024. Available from: https://en.wikipedia.org/w/index.php?title=Pomodoro_Technique&oldid=1254101879

4. Gutmann M, TEDx. Are we celebrating the wrong leaders? [Internet]. 2024 [cited 2024 Oct 30]. Available from: https://www.ted.com/talks/m artin_gutmann_ are_we_celebrating_the_wrong_leaders/

Continuous improvement

11

Progressing in the job

Careers are long. They take you to many different places and present you with many different challenges along the way. You will be solely responsible for managing the mighty project that is "Yourself"; how you will progress, meet your needs, find your challenges and land your successes over time. This chapter will explore some of the options and pursuits that may shape the evolution of your production career.

LEVELING UP – PRODUCER TITLES

The exact meaning of producer titles is as wild and varied as everything else in game production, so they are not a hard measure of skill and experience, nor an exact predictor of responsibilities.

The place where titles become most important is when applying for another job, and here is what I think they are commonly understood to connote:

- **Intern/junior/assistant producer (fairly interchangeable)** – New, inexperienced, and in the onboarding stage of their career. They will need mentoring, and their roles will mostly be about supporting another producer/senior producer in their duties, such as running meetings, managing documentation, organizing activities like playtests and reviews, and similar.

- **Associate producer** – Fairly new to production, and still very much learning the role, but should be more capable of autonomous working. They should have solid communication skills and be able to write effective reports and run effective meetings. Mentoring will still be needed. They are likely to be given one or two small teams to own and manage and possibly own a pipeline (I was given localization ownership during my time as an associate producer).
- **Producer** (aka "mid-level") – Capable and knowledgeable of all the general production practices, such as day-to-day project management, effective communication, planning, scheduling, and problem-solving. Producers should be regularly pitching improvements to team processes and contributing to how the wider team is run. Should be comfortable talking to anyone on the team.
- **Technical producer** – Less focused on management of gameplay features, and more about managing technical teams, processes, and pipeline improvements. At least the same level of experience as the producer, but will also need sufficient technical experience to be able to problem-solve in programming, build, and source control environments. They also often serve as experts in managing production software.
- **Senior producer** – Should be able to arrive and adapt to the environment with minimal onboarding, able to acquire the information needed to support the team of their own initiative. They may also be hired to bring a missing skill set to the team (e.g., managing code teams, agile methodology, outsourcing experience, etc.), in the hope that they can uplift the team's knowledge in this area. Senior producers will be expected to be capable of mentoring new producers. They may be given a large group of features, or ownership of particularly complex pipelines, or simply just lots of both. They should be regularly contributing to process evolution, suggesting new tools, and generally looking for ways to improve how the team works.
- **Lead producer** – As well as managing large clusters of feature areas the lead producer will likely be managing a group of producers; they will be direct manager to several of them and will be responsible for ensuring that their team is delivering well on production responsibilities. They will be expected to dictate the initial methodology and processes that their producers will use to manage their features, such as sprints, reports, and schedule types. A lead producer will often be the first production hire on a project and will be responsible for hiring and building the rest of the production team.

- **Production director/head of production** – Oversees all production activity on the project and is the ultimate decision-maker for team production methodology and will also be the direct manager of the lead and senior producers. They will also generally be the guardian of the team's budget and will manage the staff resource plan and allocations. This person is held to account by the executive producer.
- **Executive producer** – This is less about the team and more about the ownership of the product and project itself. This person is accountable to the external stakeholders, such as the publisher or clients. They will be responsible for balancing the priorities of the stakeholders with those of the studio, and communicating these to the various game directors, who will incorporate these into the milestone deliverables. They will also be involved with any conversations for pitching games and for negotiating and signing contracts with publishers. They will likely be involved in play-tests when it is time to approve milestone features.

PROMOTIONS AND PAY RISES

Promotions and pay rises can be a contentious topic. Some people value titles more than others, and a pay rise can have a very different significance depending on your financial situation.

Some more established studios may have clear definitions for their staff levels with specified pay brackets and criteria for promotion, while other studios are completely playing it by ear. There's no exact playbook for climbing these ladders, but here are some questions you can ask to make more sense of your environment.

Which one are you really after? The title or the money?

In some cases promotions and pay rises are not always tied together. Promotions mean changing your job title and are an agreement across the company/industry as to your skill level, responsibility level, and performance expectations, whereas a pay rise is simply about the compensation you are being given from that once particular company. In the past I have negotiated for a higher salary without a title increase, because I wanted my performance acknowledged financially, but

I wasn't looking for a change in responsibilities yet. Of course, promotions are also a key investment in your future job prospects as well, so if you are invested in climbing the production ladder, then go for the next title, but be ready for the increased expectations and responsibilities that will come with it.

Why do you want it?

Before you start negotiating for your next promotion, make sure you know why you want it, as you will find it easier to discuss your needs. Some different examples I can think of:

- Your cost-of-living circumstances have changed, and thus your salary needs have increased
- You want new responsibilities and growth in your career
- You feel you are already doing the job at the higher level
- You feel your work is more valuable to the company than your salary acknowledges
- Your salary is unfairly low compared to your peers in the company/industry

Figure out this answer for yourself before you begin, as it will help you find what you actually need.

What are your company's criteria?

Before starting any negotiations, study any criteria that your company may have for the job positions. Larger companies tend to have heavily defined criteria specs for each job position, which may include responsibilities covered, management experience, and time in the industry. If not, try to find out who makes the decisions, and how they judge when it is time to promote someone. Knowing these criteria can help you form a better argument for your promotion.

Would you leave your job over it?

If you ask for a promotion and your company says no, then this is the only real card you can play. If they say no, you will have a better chance of them reconsidering if you have an offer from another company that you want your studio to match. If your company doesn't (or can't) match that offer, then you have to decide if you're ready to move on. This might feel like playing dirty, but it really isn't; this is just everyday competition in the job market. Of course you may not want to leave your job at all, and while you should still ask for what you feel you deserve, be aware that you may not have as much luck, unless you're willing to put something on the line.

Be transparent when negotiating

Start clearly saying what you want, and be honest with your reasoning. Be courteous, and make it clear that you do want to stay at the company, and you want them to invest in keeping you. If you have other offers, then tell them up-front, as it will make your situation clear. If you have external financial needs (e.g., a new baby, a rent increase, and a family dependent), then be up-front with this as well; any transparency builds trust in you, and they will want to invest in people they trust.

Timing is important

It's worth considering *when* you open negotiations, as you don't want it to be someone's problem. Some companies have a promotion schedule and only run their promotions once or twice a year, so time your discussions in advance of these periods. Similarly, many companies will only enact pay rises at certain times of year, sometimes only at the turn of the tax year. If this is the case, make sure you ask well ahead of the pay rise date so there is time for your manager to make the change that year, if they agree. Also, if your manager is unusually busy or stressed, then it may be best to wait until it has passed, and they are perhaps feeling more charitable.

A quick summary for things to consider when negotiating a promotion or pay rise:

- **Figure out exactly what you want to ask for**
- **Understand why you're asking for it**
- **Consider your company/manager's criteria**
- **Decide if you would change job for this**
- **Negotiate honestly**
- **Time it well**

WHEN SHOULD I CHANGE JOBS?

I've changed jobs multiple times in my career, each time being driven by a mixture of factors. Here are the main ones that have been part of my decision-making at one time or another:

- No more opportunities to expand skills
- No more opportunities to expand responsibilities
- Out-of-control workload leading to burnout
- Frustrations with manager style
- Lost faith in viability of project
- A good opportunity came up on another team

Ultimately, what drives me in my own career is personal growth and development, so this has steered my decision-making. Other common motivations include increasing salary, desire for high-level titles, or wanting to work with specific teams/people/games.

When you start a role, think back to why you applied and what you want to get out of that role. Maybe it's building experience, or learning a new industry area, or working in your favorite genre. Then, if you ever start feeling frustrated, you can ask yourself if you're even getting what you came for. If you're still meeting your career goals, then maybe it's not the right time to leave, and instead better to focus on improving whatever the problem is. However, if you're frustrated, and you're not even getting what you came for anymore, then it sounds like it's time to go looking for that next step.

BIG STUDIO, LITTLE STUDIO

As you proceed in your career, you may want to think about which types of studio you want to work for. I have worked in both a company of 70 people and a globe-spanning corporation with employees numbering in the hundreds of thousands. The environments have been wildly different, with each one teaching me very different lessons, but all have helped me grow as a producer in different ways.

Here are some things to consider that vary between big and small studios:

Specialization vs generalization

In a big studio your opportunities will likely be focused on a specific aspect of your job; you may just be running a pipeline or one or two SCRUM teams on single features. You will gain a lot of experience in making a team work, but you won't learn as much about how an entire company fits together as if you are in a smaller studio, where you may well be running an entire project from start to finish, as well as handling budgets, recruitment processes, and maybe even acting as an office manager. The smaller the company, the more everyone has to chip in to different company functions, and the producer responsibilities will be most spread out of all.

Predictability vs flexibility

A game studio generally takes time to grow large, building off years of successful output. This tends to encourage the building of predictable pipelines, where each individual has their function in keeping the great machine ticking along and keeping the output up. Producers in big studios will often have incredibly long product roadmaps stretching out for years, and plan their teams and processes with these far-off goals in mind. Smaller studios are less likely to have this; there will generally be much more emphasis on the team being flexible to respond to the needs of the others, and changes in direction will be easier to arrange, as you can get the entire team in a room to discuss the idea. The mobile game industry can confuse this trend somewhat, as large mobile game companies may have rigid and defined company processes, while the projects themselves will be intensely fast-moving, dynamic, and reactive.

Comfort vs passion

Big studios want to stay big. That means retaining their staff, so they'll need to keep them comfortable. This means that bigger studios generally have higher pay, generous benefit packages, and a broad range of employee support infrastructure. Conversely, a small studio will not be able to afford the larger comfort items, and these places are usually propped up by the passion and drive of their team members; joining a small studio is often an opportunity to have a much bigger impact on the game you're making and is the reason why many veterans of big game studios break off and start their own small studio where their ideas can define the entire game, deeming it worth the risk of a harder life for a while.

Campus vs coffee shop

We can't ignore the fact that big studios will have larger offices, generally with better facilities. I worked in Microsoft's multi-building campus in Thames Valley Park which boasted two cafeterias, a crèche, on-site parking, and a lake. You won't get that in a small studio renting an office space in a city block, or maybe they're mostly remote, and only co-develop in a coffee shop. However, some people are energized by the less formalized surroundings and feel much happier working remotely or sharing a hack-space with other creatives deep in their own pursuits.

Both big studios and small studios will provide valuable lessons for a growing producer and can be extremely fulfilling life and career experiences in their own right. I personally think there is a huge value in starting your career in a larger studio; there are more peers to learn from and more infrastructure for focused learning resources like courses and training. Of course, you may be one of these people who go straight out of university into indie development with a game idea crackling in their heads and an insatiable drive to show the world their ideas right away, in which case dive in and make it happen!

Closing words – make it happen!

12

And so we reach the end of the book. I hope now you have a clearer idea of the journey ahead, and feel more equipped to navigate the ever-changing landscape of the game industry. We've talked about how you get in, who you'll meet, what challenges you'll face, and covered as many methods and tools as I have space to write about!

I could have spent the whole book telling you exactly what happened on all my projects, but what with the endless new genres, changing platforms, and evolving development tools is it likely that my exact production experiences will be out of date in no time at all, and in truth I have no idea what the games industry is going to do next. Instead, my intention with this book has been to give you the background knowledge, teach you development language, and furnish you with the questions that can help you adapt to any new situation, and how to look after yourself in the everyday chaos of game development. I have also put a lot of focus on communication, understanding, and other "people skills" in this book for a reason; games change, technologies change, and audiences change, but people skills are forever. Especially for producers.

I love my job as a game producer. I get to be surrounded by excited, passionate, intelligent people every single day, and I get to solve all the problems to help them deploy their collective genius as fast and freely as possible. Yes, it can sometimes feel like everything imaginable ends up being my job, but I relish it. The challenges never stop evolving, and I don't think I will ever get bored here.

So good luck, producer! Enjoy being that person with every job. Enjoy being someone that gets things done. Enjoy being the one that makes it happen!

DOI: 10.1201/9781003519065-12

Glossary of terms

AAA (triple-A) games – Large games with big teams and big budgets, intended to raise huge revenue.

Active Listening – A method of listening in which you proactively take steps to listen to a person, and help them expand on their thoughts by giving attention, space, and asking exploratory questions.

Agile – A set of development principles intended to optimize management of projects with regular deliveries.

(Agile) Crystal – An offshoot of Agile project management in which the quality of person-to-person interactions and communication is the main priority.

(Agile) Kanban – A method in Agile project management which defines a shared team to-do list, with defined throughput and status-tracking.

(Agile) Lean – A concept in Agile project management which focuses on removal of wasteful processes to improve team efficiency.

(Agile) SCRUM – A method in Agile project management in which development is arranged into a repeating sequence of two- to four-week "sprints" in which work is prioritized, planned, completed, and reviewed.

Bottleneck – A common metaphorical term for the slowest part of a pipeline, where the work starts to pile up because the workload is greater than the throughput.

Bug Severity – Sometimes known as "class," this is a ranking used by QA testers to communicate the impact of a bug on the plate experience, which will assist the producer in assigning a fix priority to the bug.

Call to action – The part of an email or message that tells the reader what the writer wants them to do.

Crunch – An extended period of overtime.

Day 1 patch – A game update that is applied on the very first day of the game's availability.

Decision Log – A document in which key decisions are recorded to facilitate transparency and can be referenced in retrospect.

Development kit (devkit) – A more powerful version of a computer/game console with extra features for development, testing, and debugging.

DLC – Stands for "downloadable content," referring to the game content that is released after the launch of the main game.

eSports – A common term for video game competitions with cash prizes.

Feature Creep – A common problem in game development, where suggestions get worked on without proper planning and costing, causing the size of the project to grow beyond the team's capacity to deliver it.

Gantt chart – Visual chart used to show waterfall schedules and highlight dependencies.

MIDI – Stands for "Musical Instrument Digital Interface" and is a framework for programming music in software.

MMORPG/MMO – Stands for "Massively Multiplayer Online Role-Playing Game," which is an RPG played in a consistent online world with many other players.

Outsourcing – Employing an external organization to meet a need for your project.

Paper prototype – A version of a game made with physical objects, often pen and paper, to test, iterate, and prove out game mechanics before committing to a digital environment.

Postmortem – A project retrospective activity, designed to gather and prioritize feedback from the entire development team.

PRINCE2 – A project management methodology focused on components, controls, and risk management.

RASCI Document – Stands for "Responsible, Accountable, Supporting, Consulted, Informed" – A document that details the responsibilities of all areas of a project.

Retrospectives – Events in which a team reflects on recent working practice and suggests improvements.

Risk Register – A document in which risks are clearly written out to enable the planning of mitigations.

R&D – Stands for "research and development," and often refers to work that is focused on innovation, technology creation, and anything else that can improve the capabilities of the team.

RPG – Stands for "role-playing game," a genre where players can evolve their characters' traits, abilities, and appearance over time.

Shooter – Short-hand for "first-person shooter," a genre of games in which the primary gameplay is firing guns.

Story Points – A method of estimating task effort, used to prioritize and plan work in agile development.

Tile-matching game – A game in which the player shuffles tiles around to match the colors or patterns for points.

Triage – A process of reviewing and prioritizing a body of work. Commonly used for backlogs, bugs, and service tickets, among other workloads.

UX – Stands for "User Experience," and refers to the discipline of designing intuitive and accessible user interfaces and interactions.

Waterfall – A project management methodology focused on managing dependencies.

XR – An umbrella term for technologies and experiences relating to VR, AR, and MR.

(XR) Augmented reality (AR) – Technology that applies digital elements to a live camera feed.

(XR) Mixed reality (MR) – Combines the real-world elements of AR with the digital interactions of VR.

(XR) Virtual reality (VR) – Fully digital environments in which the user's eyes are fully enclosed, often involving tracking devices on their body to enable physical control.

Recommended Reading

The Culture Map: Breaking Through the Invisible Boundaries of Global Business – Erin Meyer. Published May 27, 2014 by PublicAffairs (New York City, NY, USA)

The Design of Everyday Things – Don Norman. Published September 19, 2002 by Basic Books (New York City, NY, USA)

Don't Make Me Think – Steve Krug. Published December 24, 2013 by New Riders (Indianapolis, IN, USA)

The Game Production Toolbox – Heather Maxwell Chandler. Published April 24, 2020 by CRC Press (Boca Raton, FL, USA)

Nine Lies about Work: A Freethinking Leader's Guide to the Real World – Ashley Goodall, Marcus Buckingham. Published April 2, 2019 by Harvard Business Review Press (Brighton, MA, USA)

Nonviolent Communication: A Language of Life – Marshall B. Rosenberg. Published September 1, 2003 by Puddledancer Press (Encinitas, CA, USA)

The Personal MBA: Master the Art of Business – Josh Kaufman. Published December 30, 2010 by Portfolio. (New York City, NY, USA)

Turn the Ship Around! A True Story of Turning Followers into Leaders – L. David Marquet. Published May 16, 2013 by Portfolio (New York City, NY, USA)